Year-Round Quilting
with *Patrick Lose*

24+ Projects to Celebrate the Seasons

Fons&Porter
Cincinnati, Ohio

Contents

Introduction

Quilters love to celebrate seasons, holidays and special occasions with their quilted treasures and I think you'll agree that *Year-Round Quilts with Patrick Lose* offers lots of ideas for doing just that. We've gathered 24 of my favorite projects from the pages of *Quilting Celebrations* magazine to inspire you to create pieces that make every day a special occasion.

There's something for everyone and for every skill level in this collection of seasonal projects. Easy piecing and simple, fusible appliqué make quick work of most of them and you're sure to make good use of all of those stash fabrics you've been saving for something special.

If you need a little help mastering the methods used in these projects, you can rely on the easy-to-follow lessons and tutorials at the end of the book. These are some of my most popular and requested techniques offered in the classes I teach. I hope you'll find them useful in strengthening your quilting skills.

Thanks so much for making my designs a part of your seasons, holidays and special occasions. I hope you enjoy all of your quilting celebrations.

Cheers!

Make this exuberant banner to ring in the New Year.

CHEERS *banner*

Size: 12" × 36"

MATERIALS

½ yard black print

¼ yard orange print

1 fat eighth* blue print

1 fat eighth* green print

1 fat eighth* pink print

1 fat eighth* yellow print

Paper-backed fusible web

⅜ yard backing fabric

16" × 40" piece of quilt batting

*fat eighth = 9" × 20"

Sew Smart™

Add a sleeve to the back of the banner for easy hanging. Refer to the Techniques section for instructions.—Patrick

Sew Smart™

Use tear-away stabilizer under your work to stabilize the banner when doing machine satin stitching.—Patrick

Cutting

Measurements include ¼" seam allowances. Follow manufacturer's instructions for using fusible web.

FROM BLACK PRINT, CUT:

- 3 (2¼"-wide) strips for binding.
- 1 (8½" × 36½") B rectangle.

FROM ORANGE PRINT, CUT:

- 1 (4½" × 36½") A rectangle.

FROM BLUE PRINT, CUT:

- 1 C.
- 1 E.
- 1 R.

FROM GREEN PRINT, CUT:

- 1 H.
- 1 E.
- 1 S.

FROM PINK PRINT, CUT:

- 3 Diamonds.

FROM YELLOW PRINT, CUT:

- 3 Diamonds.

Banner Assembly

1 Join orange print A rectangle and black print B rectangle as shown in Quilt Top Assembly Diagrams to make banner background.

2 Referring to Quilt Top Assembly Diagrams, arrange appliqué pieces on banner background; fuse in place.

3 Machine appliqué using satin stitch. Letters are stitched using matching thread. Diamonds are stitched with pink thread.

4 Satin stitch diamond pattern on diamond section using orange thread.

Finishing

1 Layer backing, batting, and quilt top; baste. Quilt as desired.

2 Add binding to quilt.

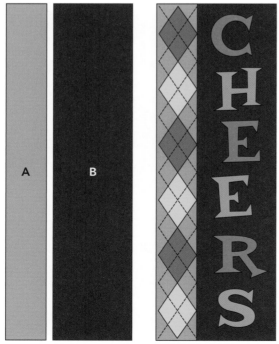

Quilt Top Assembly Diagrams

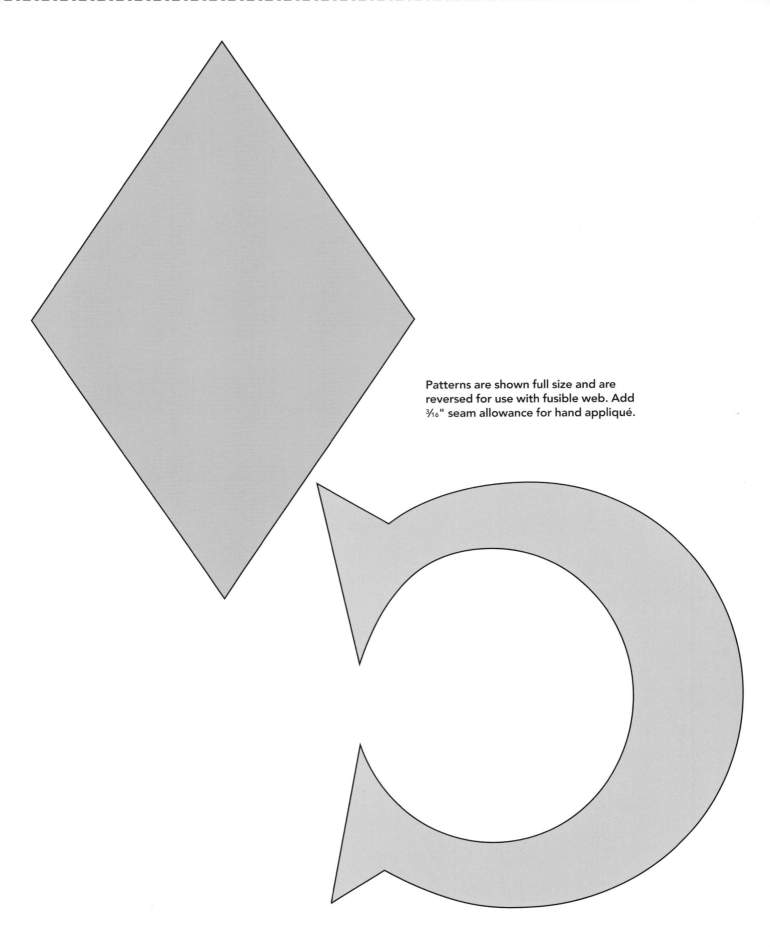

Patterns are shown full size and are reversed for use with fusible web. Add $\frac{3}{16}$" seam allowance for hand appliqué.

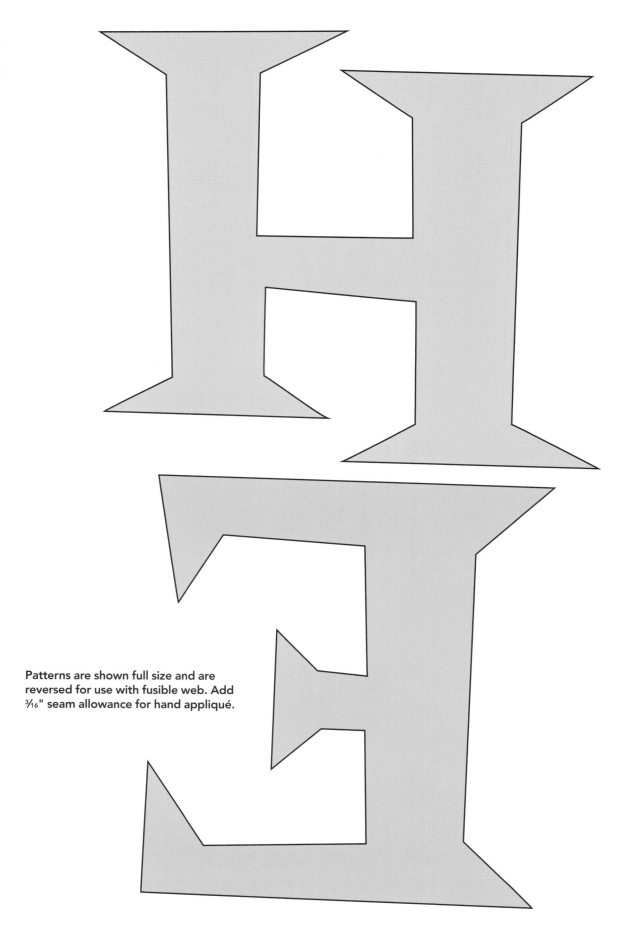

Patterns are shown full size and are
reversed for use with fusible web. Add
³⁄₁₆" seam allowance for hand appliqué.

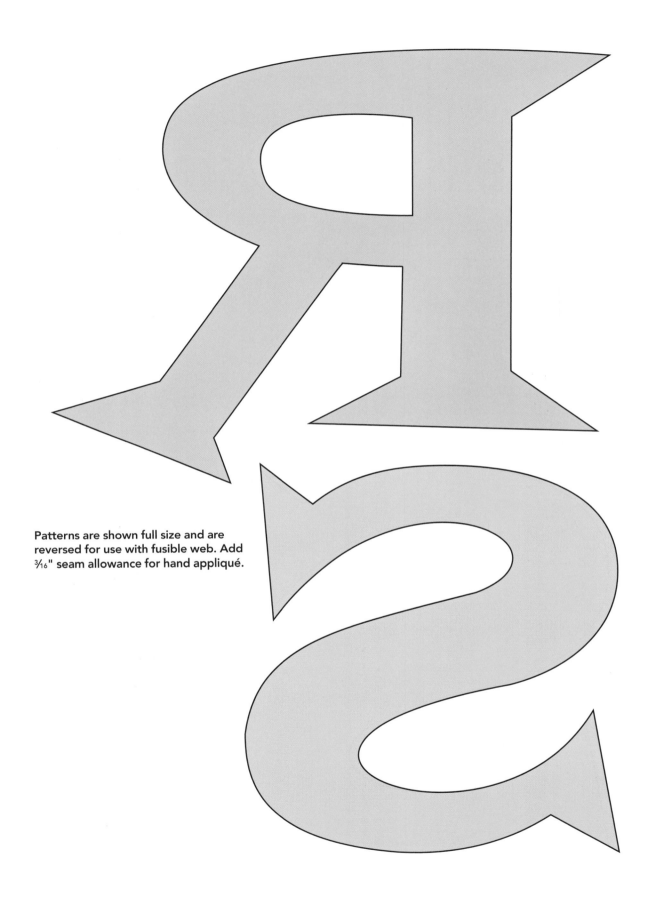

Patterns are shown full size and are reversed for use with fusible web. Add ³/₁₆" seam allowance for hand appliqué.

Choose groupings of warm and cool colors from your stash to build these blocks inspired by contemporary stained glass windows.

CHAPEL WINDOWS *quilt*

Size: 75" × 75"
Blocks: 25 (9") blocks

MATERIALS

2 yards black print for blocks and sashing

2½ yards blue print for blocks, border, and binding

⅜ yard light blue print for blocks

⅝ yard green print for blocks and sashing

½ yard purple print for blocks

⅝ yard yellow print for blocks and sashing

⅜ yard orange print for blocks

½ yard red print for blocks

½ yard dark red print for blocks

4¾ yards backing fabric

Full-size quilt batting

Cutting

Measurements include ¼" seam allowances. Border strips are exact length needed. You may want to make them longer to allow for piecing variations.

FROM BLACK PRINT, CUT:

- 18 (3½"-wide) strips. From strips, cut 60 (3½" × 9½") sashing rectangles and 25 (3½") F squares.

FROM BLUE PRINT, CUT:

- 8 (6½"-wide) strips. Piece strips to make 2 (6½" × 75½") top and bottom borders and 2 (6½" × 63½") side borders.

- 2 (3½"-wide) strips. From strips, cut 24 (3½" × 2¾") E rectangles.

- 8 (2¼"-wide) strips for binding.

- 3 (2"-wide) strips. From strips, cut 24 (2" × 2¾") B rectangles and 12 (2" × 2½") I rectangles.

FROM LIGHT BLUE PRINT, CUT:

- 1 (3½"-wide) strip. From strip, cut 12 (3½" × 2¾") E rectangles.

- 3 (2"-wide) strips. From strips, cut 12 (2" × 3½") D rectangles and 24 (2") C squares.

FROM GREEN PRINT, CUT:

- 9 (2"-wide) strips. From 5 strips, cut 12 (2" × 4¼") A rectangles, 24 (2" × 2¾") B rectangles, 12 (2") C squares, and 12 (2" × 1¼") J rectangles. Remaining strips are for strip sets.

FROM PURPLE PRINT, CUT:

- 1 (3½"-wide) strip. From strip, cut 12 (3½" × 1¼") G rectangles.

- 4 (2"-wide) strips. From strips, cut 12 (2" × 4½") H rectangles and 24 (2" × 3½") D rectangles.

FROM YELLOW PRINT, CUT:

- 9 (2"-wide) strips. From 5 strips, cut 13 (2" × 4¼") A rectangles, 26 (2" × 2¾") B rectangles, 13 (2") C squares, and 13 (2" × 1¼") J rectangles. Remaining strips are for strip sets.

FROM ORANGE PRINT, CUT:

- 1 (3½"-wide) strip. From strip, cut 13 (3½" × 2¾") E rectangles.

- 3 (2"-wide) strips. From strips, cut 13 (2" × 3½") D rectangles and 26 (2") C squares.

FROM PURPLE PRINT, CUT:

- 1 (3½"-wide) strip. From strip, cut 12 (3½" × 1¼") G rectangles.

- 4 (2"-wide) strips. From strips, cut 12 (2" × 4½") H rectangles and 24 (2" × 3½") D rectangles.

FROM RED PRINT, CUT:

- 2 (3½"-wide) strips. From strips, cut 26 (3½" × 2¾") E rectangles.

- 3 (2"-wide) strips. From strips, cut 26 (2" × 2¾") B rectangles and 12 (2" × 2½") I rectangles.

FROM DARK RED PRINT, CUT:

- 1 (3½"-wide) strip. From strip, cut 13 (3½" × 1¼") G rectangles.

- 4 (2"-wide) strips. From strips, cut 13 (2" × 4½") H rectangles and 26 (2" x 3½") D rectangles.

Block Assembly

1 Lay out 1 set of block pieces as shown in Block Assembly Diagrams.

2 Join into sections; join sections to complete 1 red block (Block Diagrams). Make 13 red blocks.

3 In the same manner, make 12 blue blocks.

MAKE 13

MAKE 12

Block Diagrams

Quilt Assembly

1 Lay out blocks, black print sashing rectangles, and Four Patch Units as shown in Quilt Top Assembly Diagram.

2 Join into rows; join rows to complete quilt center.

3 Add blue print side borders to the quilt center. Add top and bottom borders to the quilt.

Finishing

1 Divide backing into 2 (2⅜-yard) lengths. Cut 1 piece in half lengthwise to make 2 narrow panels. Join 1 narrow panel to each side of wider panel; press seam allowances toward narrow panels.

2 Layer backing, batting, and quilt top; baste. Quilt as desired.

3 Join 2¼"-wide blue print strips into 1 continuous piece for straight-grain French-fold binding. Add binding to quilt.

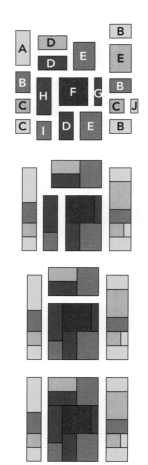

Block Assembly Diagrams

Sashing Assembly

1 Join 1 yellow print strip and 1 green print strip as shown in Strip Set Diagram. Make 4 strip sets.

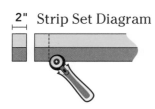

2" Strip Set Diagram

2 From strip sets, cut 72 (2"-wide) segments.

3 Join 2 segments as shown in Four Patch Unit Diagrams. Make 36 Four Patch Units.

Four Patch Unit Diagrams

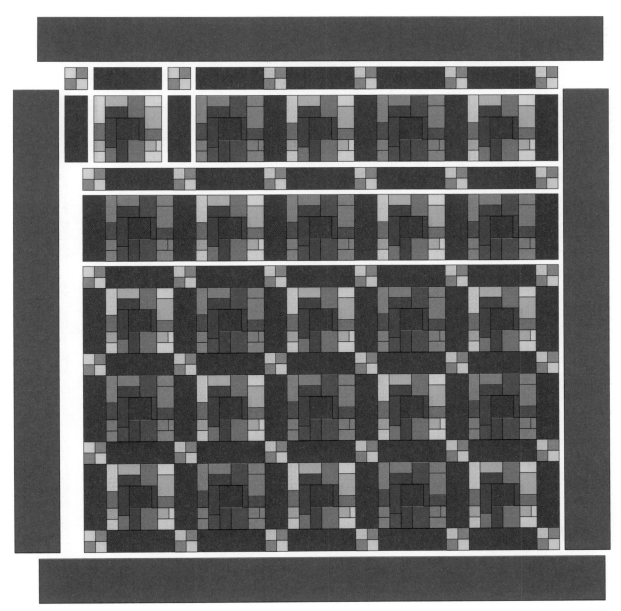

Quilt Top Assembly Diagram

Appliqué hearts on this terrific table topper for your Valentine. You can embroider them by hand or machine.

PRETTY IN PINKS *table topper*

Size: 20" diameter

MATERIALS

⅝ yard ivory print

1 fat quarter* blossom print

1 fat eighth** petal print

Paper-backed fusible web

Pink perle cotton

⅝ yard backing fabric

24" square quilt batting

*fat quarter = 18" × 20"

**fat eighth = 9" × 20"

Web Extra

A digitized file for Heart Scroll design for machine embroidery is available at www.patricklose.com.

Sew Smart™

If you are using the digitized embroidery file, follow instructions included for stitching order. —Patrick

Cutting

Measurements include ¼" seam allowances. Follow manufacturer's instructions for using fusible web.

FROM IVORY PRINT, CUT:

- 1 Table Topper background.

FROM BLOSSOM PRINT, CUT:

- 4 Large Hearts.
- 80" of 2¼"-wide bias strips. Join strips to make bias binding.

FROM PETAL PRINT, CUT:

- 4 Small Hearts.

Table Topper Assembly

1 Referring to photo on page 19, arrange hearts atop ivory print background. Fuse pieces in place.

2 Machine appliqué using satin stitch and matching thread.

3 Trace Heart Scroll designs on background. Using pink perle cotton, backstitch designs (Backstitch Diagram, page 18).

Finishing

1 Layer backing, batting, and quilt top; baste. Quilt as desired.

2 Add binding to quilt.

Sew Smart™

Use tear-away stabilizer under your work to stabilize the topper when doing machine satin stitching.—Patrick

Backstitch Diagram

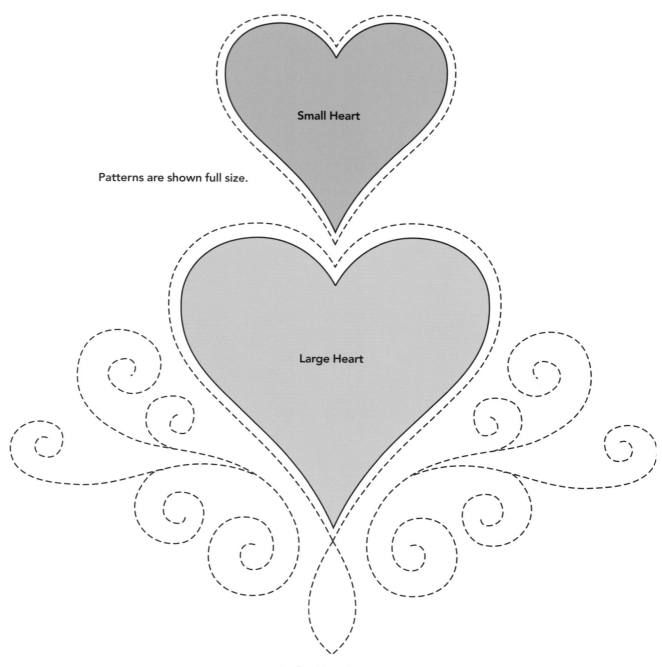

Small Heart

Patterns are shown full size.

Large Heart

Embroidery Pattern

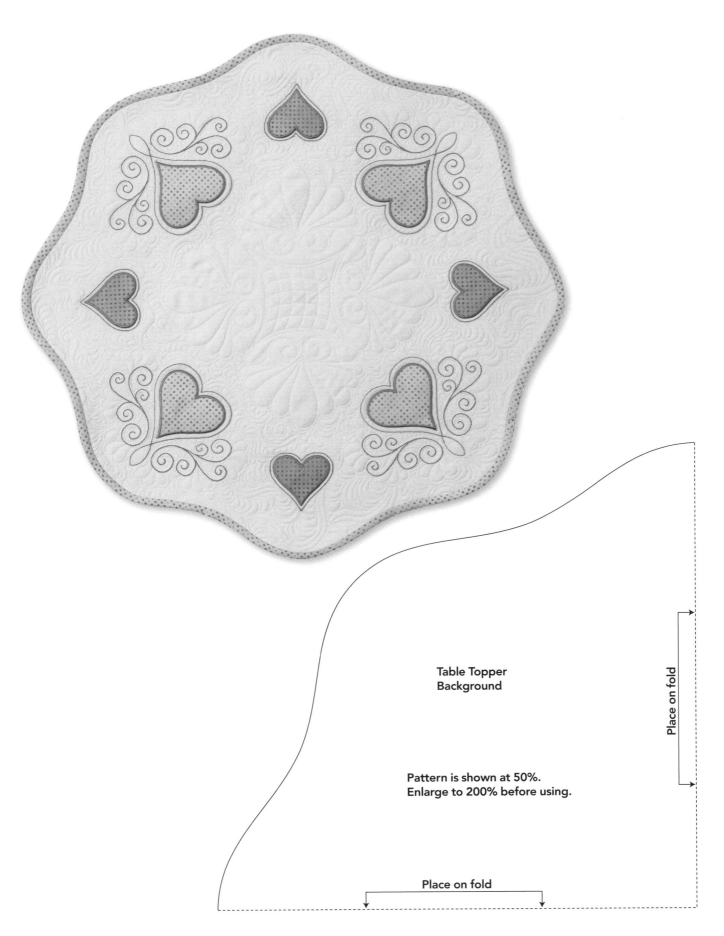

**Table Topper
Background**

Pattern is shown at 50%.
Enlarge to 200% before using.

Place on fold

Place on fold

Cute, contemporary prints in bright colors make this pillow a great Valentine's Day gift or year-round accessory.

HUGS & KISSES *pillow*

Size: 20½" × 20½"

MATERIALS

1 fat quarter* white print #1

1 yard white print #2

½ yard pink print

1 fat quarter* green print

1½ yards backing fabric

Paper-backed fusible web

22"-square pillow form

Craft-size quilt batting

*fat quarter = 18" × 20"

Cutting

Measurements include ¼" seam allowances. Follow manufacturer's instructions for using fusible web.

FROM WHITE PRINT #1, CUT:

- 1 (4½"-wide) strip. From strip, cut 4 (4½") squares.
- 1 Heart.
- 4 Os.

FROM WHITE PRINT #2, CUT:

- 1 (21"-wide) strip. From strip, cut 2 (21" × 13") rectangles.
- 2 (4"-wide) strips. From strips, cut 2 (4" × 21") top and bottom outer borders and 2 (4" × 14") side outer borders.

FROM PINK PRINT, CUT:

- 1 (4½"-wide) strip. From strip, cut 5 (4½") squares.
- 5 (2¼"-wide) strips for binding.
- 4 Xs.

FROM GREEN PRINT, CUT:

- 4 (1¼"-wide) strips. From strips, cut 2 (1¼" × 14") top and bottom inner borders and 2 (1¼" × 12½") side inner borders.

FROM BACKING FABRIC, CUT:

- 2 (24"-wide) strips. From strips, cut 1 (24") square and 2 (24" × 16") rectangles.

FROM BATTING, CUT:

- 1 (24") square.
- 2 (24" × 16") rectangles.

Pillow Top Assembly

1 Position appliqué pieces on white print #1 and pink print background squares as shown in photo; fuse in place.

2 Machine appliqué using matching thread and satin stitch.

3 Lay out appliquéd squares as shown in Assembly Diagram. Join into rows; join rows to complete center.

4 Add green print side inner borders to center. Add green print top and bottom inner borders to center.

5 Repeat for white print #2 outer borders.

6 Layer bordered square, batting square, and front backing square; baste. Quilt as desired.

7 Trim batting and backing even with edges of bordered square.

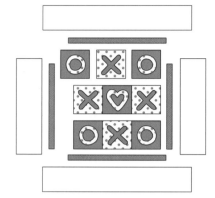

Assembly Diagram

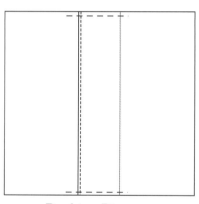

Backing Diagram

Finishing

1 Layer 1 white print #2 rectangle, 1 batting rectangle, and 1 backing rectangle; baste. Quilt as desired.

2 Trim batting and backing even with edges of white rectangle.

3 Add binding to 1 long edge of quilted back rectangle.

4 Make 2 back rectangles.

5 Overlap bound edges of back rectangles, making back square the same size as pillow top. Baste overlapped edges together (Backing Diagram).

6 Place pillow top atop back square, wrong sides facing. Baste around outer edge.

7 Add binding to pillow.

8 Insert pillow form into pillow cover.

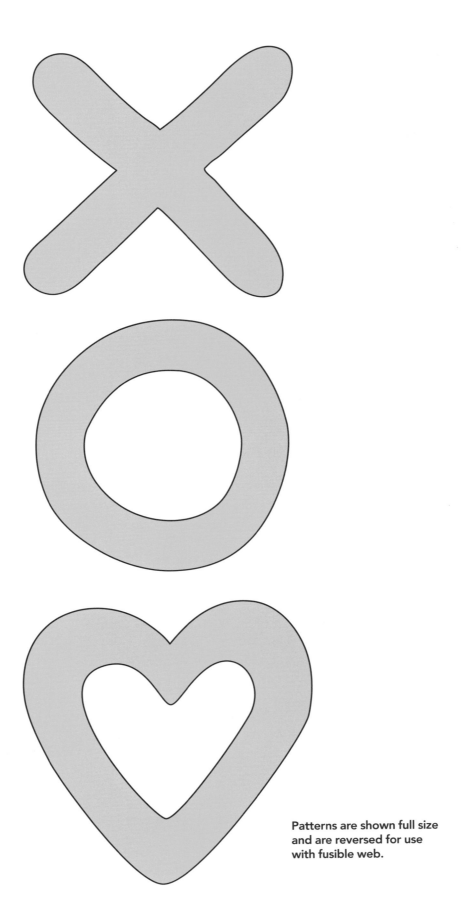

Patterns are shown full size
and are reversed for use
with fusible web.

Bright colors and a whimsical design make this placemat a great early spring table accessory. It's the perfect size for trying out a technique that's new to you.

LOVEBIRDS *placemat*

Size: 18" × 14"

MATERIALS

½ yard dark blue print

1 fat quarter* medium blue print

1 fat quarter* light blue print

1 fat quarter* pink print

Paper-backed fusible web

1 fat quarter* backing fabric

18" × 20" rectangle quilt batting

*fat quarter = 18" × 20"

Cutting

Measurements include ¼" seam allowances. Follow manufacturer's instructions for using fusible web.

FROM DARK BLUE PRINT, CUT:

- 2 (2¼"-wide) strips for binding.
- 1 (12½" × 14½") A rectangle.

FROM MEDIUM BLUE PRINT, CUT:

- 1 (2½"-wide) strip. From strip, cut 8 (2½") B squares.
- 1 Bird.
- 1 Bird reversed.

FROM LIGHT BLUE PRINT, CUT:

- 2 (2½"-wide) strips. From strips, cut 10 (2½") B squares.
- 1 Wing.
- 1 Wing reversed.

FROM PINK PRINT, CUT:

- 1 (2½"-wide) strip. From strip, cut 3 (2½") B squares.
- 1 Heart.

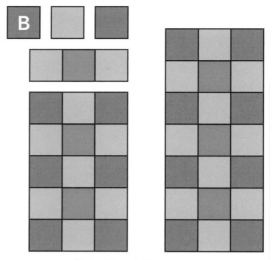

Side Unit Diagrams

Mat Assembly

1 Lay out B squares as shown in Side Unit Diagrams. Join squares into rows; join rows to make Side Unit.

2 Add Side Unit to dark blue print A rectangle as shown in Background Assembly Diagram.

3 Arrange appliqué pieces on background as shown in photo; fuse in place.

4 Machine appliqué using satin stitch and matching thread.

5 Stitch bird beaks and legs using yellow thread. Stitch tail feathers using blue thread. Stitch eyes using black thread.

Finishing

1 Layer backing, batting, and quilt top; baste. Quilt as desired. Quilt shown was quilted with overall meandering using variegated thread (Quilting Diagram).

2 Join 2¼"-wide dark blue print strips into 1 continuous piece for straight-grain French-fold binding. Add binding to quilt.

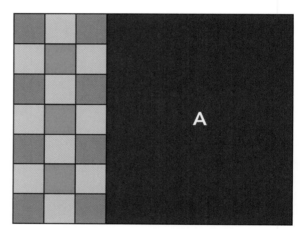

Background Assembly Diagram

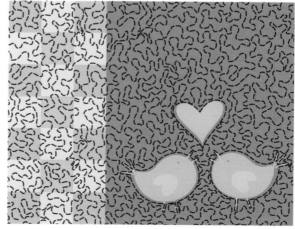

Quilting Diagram

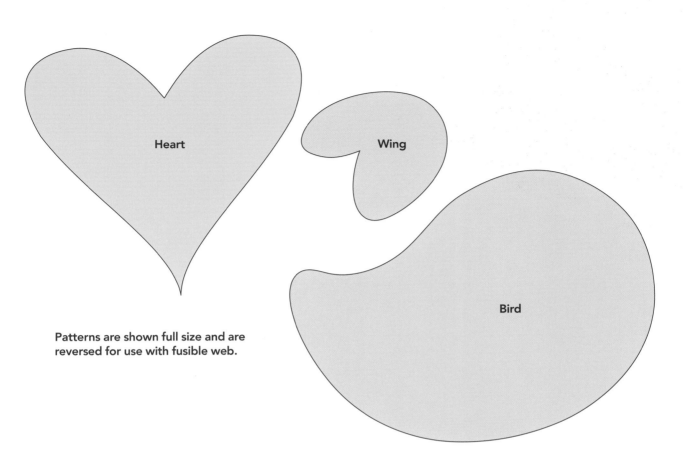

Heart

Wing

Bird

Patterns are shown full size and are reversed for use with fusible web.

Nine easy-to-piece blocks are combined in a tulip-themed throw that's perfect for a picnic.

TULIP GARDEN *throw*

Size: 62" × 62"
Blocks: 9 (18") blocks

MATERIALS

1½ yards turquoise print for blocks

1 yard raspberry print for blocks

¾ yard orange print for blocks

1½ yards grape print for sashing and binding

¾ yard lime print for blocks

Fons & Porter Half & Quarter ruler (optional)

4 yards backing fabric

Twin-size quilt batting

Cutting

Measurements include ¼" seam allowances. Instructions are written for using the Fons & Porter Half & Quarter Ruler. For instructions on using this ruler, go to www.FonsandPorter.com/chst. If not using this ruler, follow cutting notes.

FROM TURQUOISE PRINT, CUT:

- 6 (4½"-wide) strips. From strips, cut 72 half-square A triangles.

Note: If not using the Fons & Porter Half & Quarter Ruler, cut 5 (4⅞"-wide) strips. From strips, cut 36 (4⅞") squares. Cut squares in half diagonally to make 72 half-square A triangles.

- 8 (2½"-wide) strips. From strips, cut 36 (2½" × 4½") D rectangles and 36 (2½") C squares.

FROM RASPBERRY PRINT, CUT:

- 6 (4½"-wide) strips. From strips, cut 40 half-square A triangles and 20 (4½") B squares.

Note: If not using the Fons & Porter Half & Quarter Ruler to cut A triangles, cut 3 (4⅞"-wide) strips. From strips, cut 20 (4⅞") squares. Cut squares in half diagonally to make 40 half-square A triangles.

- 2 (2½"-wide) strips. From strips, cut 20 (2½") C squares.

FROM ORANGE PRINT, CUT:

- 4 (4½"-wide) strips. From strips, cut 32 half-square A triangles and 16 (4½") B squares.

Note: If not using the Fons & Porter Half & Quarter Ruler to cut A triangles, cut 2 (4⅞"-wide) strips. From strips, cut 16 (4⅞") squares. Cut squares in half diagonally to make 32 half-square A triangles.

- 1 (2½"-wide) strip. From strip, cut 16 (2½") C squares.

FROM GRAPE PRINT, CUT:

- 12 (2½"-wide) strips. From strips, cut 24 (2½" × 18½") sashing rectangles and 9 (2½") C squares.

- 7 (2¼"-wide) strips for binding.

FROM LIME PRINT, CUT:

- 10 (2½"-wide) strips. From strips, cut 36 (2½" × 8½") E rectangles and 16 (2½") C squares.

Block Assembly

1 Join 1 turquoise print A triangle and 1 raspberry print A triangle as shown in Triangle-Square Diagrams. Make 40 raspberry triangle-squares.

MAKE 40   MAKE 32

Triangle Square Diagrams

2 In the same manner, make 32 orange triangle-squares using turquoise print and orange print A triangles.

3 Join 1 raspberry print C square, 1 turquoise print C square, and 1 turquoise print D rectangle as shown in Unit 1 Assembly Diagrams. Make 20 raspberry Unit 1.

4 In the same manner, make 16 orange Unit 1 using 1 turquoise print C square, 1 turquoise print D rectangle, and 1 orange print C square in each.

5 Join 2 raspberry triangle-squares, 1 raspberry Unit 1, and 1 raspberry print B square as shown in Block Unit Diagrams. Make 20 raspberry Block Units.

6 In the same manner, make 16 orange Block Units using 2 orange triangle-squares, 1 orange print B square, and 1 orange Unit 1 in each.

7 Lay out 4 matching block Units, 4 lime print E rectangles, and 1 grape print C square as shown in Block Assembly Diagram. Join into rows; join rows to complete 1 block (Block Diagrams). Make 9 blocks in colors as shown.

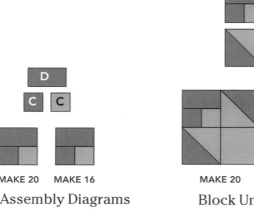

Unit 1 Assembly Diagrams

MAKE 20   MAKE 16

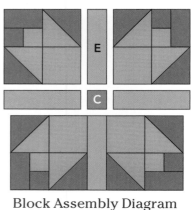

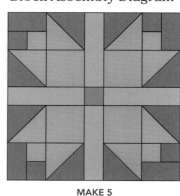

MAKE 20   MAKE 16

Block Unit Diagrams

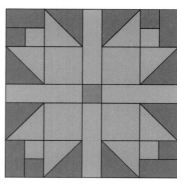

Block Assembly Diagram

MAKE 5

MAKE 4

Block Diagrams

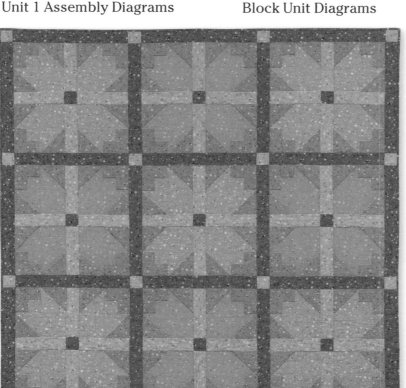

Quilt Top Assembly Diagram

Quilt Assembly

1 Lay out blocks, grape print sashing rectangles, and lime print C squares as shown in Quilt Top Assembly Diagram.

2 Join into rows; join rows to complete quilt top.

Finishing

1 Divide backing into 2 (2-yard) lengths. Cut 1 piece in half lengthwise to make 2 narrow panels. Join 1 narrow panel to each side of wider panel; press seam allowances toward narrow panels.

2 Layer backing, batting, and quilt top; baste. Quilt as desired. Quilt shown was quilted with feather designs in the blocks, and scroll designs in sashing.

3 Join 2¼"-wide grape print strips into 1 continuous piece for straight-grain French-fold binding. Add binding to quilt.

Butterfiles are in bloom and it's time to bring on the brights! Set your spring table with this quick and easy centerpiece. We bet you'll want to make more than one!

SPRING BUTTERFLIES *mini mat*

Size: approximately 12" diameter

MATERIALS

1 fat quarter* blue print for background

10" square yellow print

1 fat quarter* orange print

Paper-backed fusible web

1 fat quarter* backing fabric

14" square quilt batting

Variegated pearl cotton in orange and yellow

16 (⅜"-diameter) light orange buttons

8 (¼"-diameter) dark orange buttons

*fat quarter = 18" × 20"

Cutting

Measurements include ¼" seam allowances. Follow manufacturer's instructions for using fusible web.

FROM BLUE PRINT FAT QUARTER, CUT:

• 1 Background.

FROM YELLOW PRINT, CUT:

• 4 Wings.

FROM ORANGE PRINT FAT QUARTER, CUT:

• 4 Bodies.

• 42" of (2¼"-wide) bias strips for binding. Join strips to make bias binding.

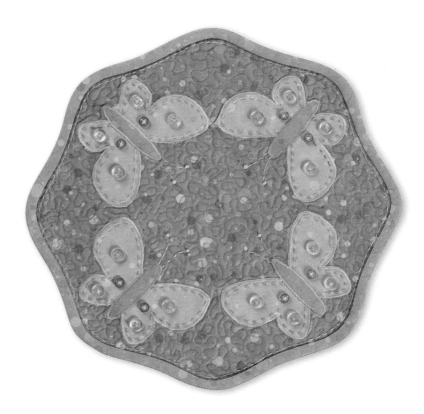

Mat Assembly

1 Arrange appliqué pieces atop blue print background as shown in photo on page 33 Fuse pieces in place.

2 Machine appliqué pieces using matching thread and satin stitch.

3 Stitch inside of wings using running stitch and orange variegated pearl cotton. Stitch antennae using running stitch and French knots at ends with yellow pearl cotton (Photos 1–3).

Finishing

1 Layer backing, batting, and mini mat top; baste. Quilt as desired. Mat shown was quilted with meandering on the blue background (Quilting Diagram).

2 Add binding to mini mat.

3 Stitch around edge of mat using a running stitch and yellow pearl cotton.

4 Referring to photo on page 33 sew buttons on wings.

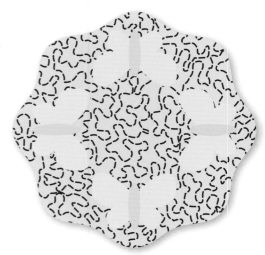

Quilting Diagram

French Knot

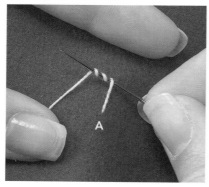

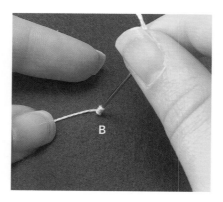

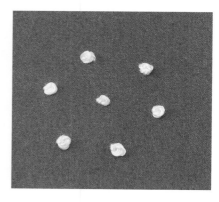

1 Bring needle to right side of fabric at A. Wrap thread around needle 2 or 3 times, keeping needle near the fabric surface.

2 Insert needle at B, right beside A. Holding the thread to keep loops wrapped around needle, gently pull thread through the loops to form a knot.

3 Repeat to make desired number of French knots. Secure thread on back side by making a shallow knot.

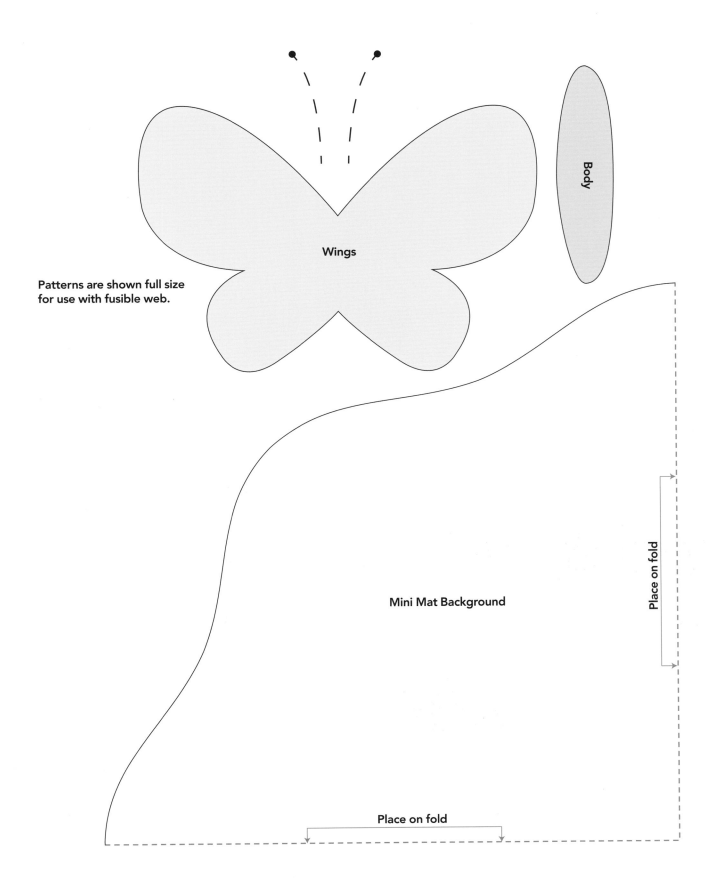

Body

Wings

Patterns are shown full size
for use with fusible web.

Mini Mat Background

Place on fold

Place on fold

Here's a cute and colorful decoration for any birthday celebration.

HAPPY BIRTHDAY *banner*

Size: 12" × 18"

MATERIALS

1 fat quarter* dark turquoise print

1 fat quarter* light turquoise print

1 fat quarter* green print

12" square cream print

8" square yellow print

8" square lavender print

4" square dark pink print

4" square light pink print

Paper-backed fusible web

1 fat quarter* backing fabric

14" × 20" piece of quilt batting

*fat quarter = 18" × 20"

Cutting

Measurements include ¼" seam allowances. Follow manufacturer's instructions for using fusible web.

FROM DARK TURQUOISE PRINT, CUT:

- 1 (8½" × 18½") rectangle.
- 1 Half Circle.
- 1 H.
- 1 A.
- 2 Ps.
- 1 Y.

FROM LIGHT TURQUOISE PRINT, CUT:

- 64" of 2¼"-wide bias strips. Join strips to make bias binding.
- 1 Candle Glow.

FROM GREEN PRINT, CUT:

- 1 (4½" × 18½#") rectangle.

FROM YELLOW PRINT, CUT:

- 1 Cake Stand.
- 1 Flame.
- 3 Flower Centers.

FROM LAVENDER PRINT, CUT:

- 1 Bow.
- 1 Candle.
- 1 set of Icing pieces.

FROM DARK PINK PRINT, CUT:

- 1 Large Flower.
- 1 Small Flower.

FROM LIGHT PINK PRINT, CUT:

- 1 Large Flower.
- 1 Inner Flame.

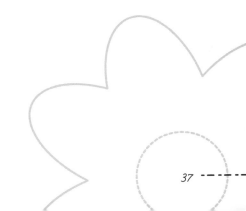

Banner Assembly

1 Join green and dark turquoise print rectangles as shown in Background Diagrams.

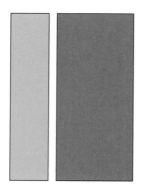

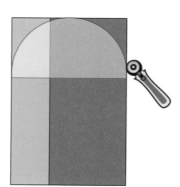

Background Diagrams

2 Trim top edge of pieced background rectangle as shown, using Half Circle template as a guide.

3 Arrange appliqué pieces on background as shown in photo; fuse in place.

4 Machine appliqué using satin stitch and matching thread. Stitch cake and bow details using satin stitch.

Finishing

1 Layer backing, batting, and quilt top; baste. Quilt as desired.

2 Trim backing and batting even with edges of quilt top.

3 Hem straight edge of dark turquoise print half circle. Baste half circle to back of quilt, aligning curved edges as shown in Back Diagram.

4 Add binding to quilt.

Back Diagram

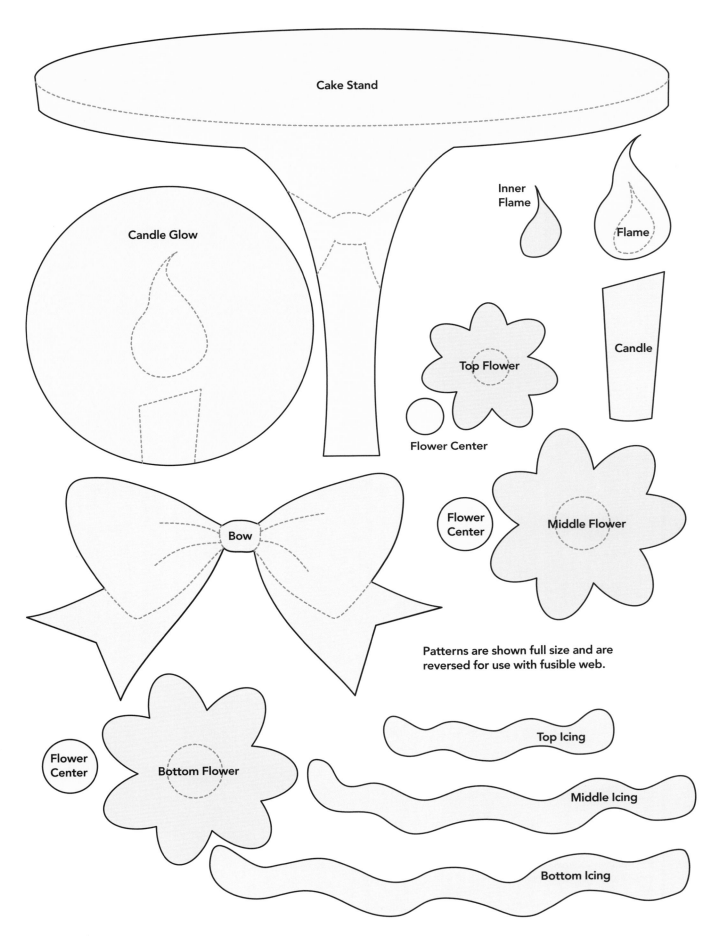

Cake Stand

Inner Flame

Flame

Candle Glow

Candle

Top Flower

Flower Center

Bow

Flower Center

Middle Flower

Patterns are shown full size and are reversed for use with fusible web.

Flower Center

Bottom Flower

Top Icing

Middle Icing

Bottom Icing

Cake

Patterns are shown full
size and are reversed for
use with fusible web.

Pattern is shown
at 50%. Enlarge to
200% before using.

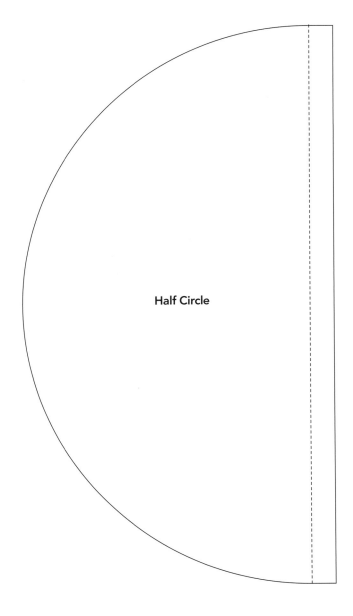

Half Circle

Use school colors and a motivational message to inspire your graduate to greatness.

A GIFT FOR THE GRAD *banner*

Size: 15" × 30"

MATERIALS

⅝ yard royal print for background and binding

1 fat quarter* blue print for borders

1 fat quarter* aqua print for hand and letters

1 fat quarter* tangerine print for border and stars

1 fat quarter* marigold print for letters and stars

Paper-backed fusible web

½ yard backing fabric

20" × 36" piece of quilt batting

*fat quarter = 18" × 20"

Cutting

Measurements include ¼" seam allowances. Follow manufacturer's instructions for using fusible web.

FROM ROYAL PRINT, CUT:

- 1 (11" × 26") A rectangle.
- 3 (2¼"-wide) strips for binding.
- 1 "4."

FROM BLUE PRINT, CUT:

- 1 (5" × 16½") B rectangle.
- 1 (5" × 11") C rectangle.

FROM AQUA PRINT, CUT:

- 1 Hand.
- 1 "re."
- 1 "ach."
- 1 "sta."
- 1 "rs."

FROM TANGERINE PRINT, CUT:

- 1 (5" × 14½") D rectangle.
- 1 Large Star.
- 1 Medium Star.
- 1 Small Star.

FROM MARIGOLD PRINT, CUT:

- 1 "t."
- 1 "h."
- 1 "e."
- 1 Medium Star.
- 1 Small Star.

Banner Assembly

1 Referring to Quilt Top Assembly Diagrams on the following page, fuse Hand to royal print A rectangle.

2 Join A rectangle, blue print B and C rectangles, and tangerine print D rectangle to make pieced background.

3 Arrange remaining appliqué pieces on background, referring to photo on page 44 for placement; fuse in place.

4 Machine appliqué using satin stitch and matching thread.

Sew Smart™

Use tear-away stabilizer under your work to stabilize the banner when doing machine satin stitching.—Patrick

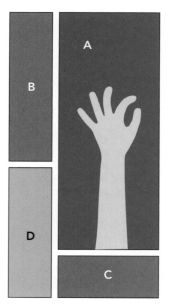 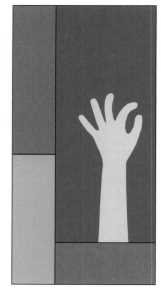 

Quilt Top Assembly Diagrams

Finishing

1 Layer backing, batting, and quilt top; baste.

2 Quilt as desired. Quilt shown was quilted around appliqué and with meandering in background and Hand.

3 Join 2¼"-wide royal strips into 1 continuous piece for straight-grain French-fold binding. Add binding to quilt.

Sew Smart™

Add a sleeve to the back of banner for easy hanging. Refer to Techniques section at the end of the book for instructions.—Patrick

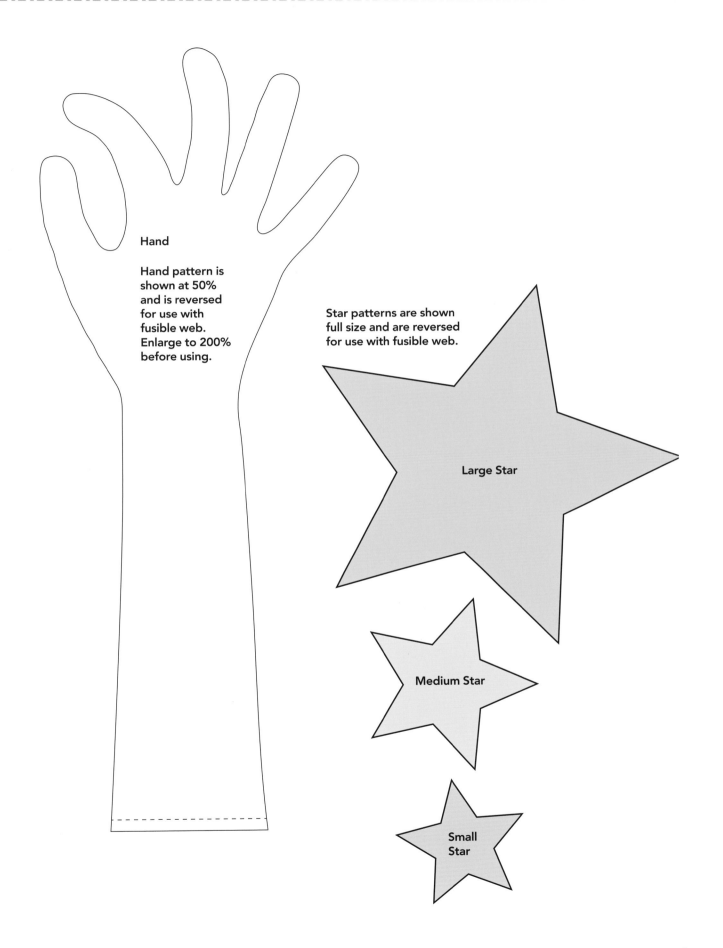

Hand

Hand pattern is shown at 50% and is reversed for use with fusible web. Enlarge to 200% before using.

Star patterns are shown full size and are reversed for use with fusible web.

Large Star

Medium Star

Small Star

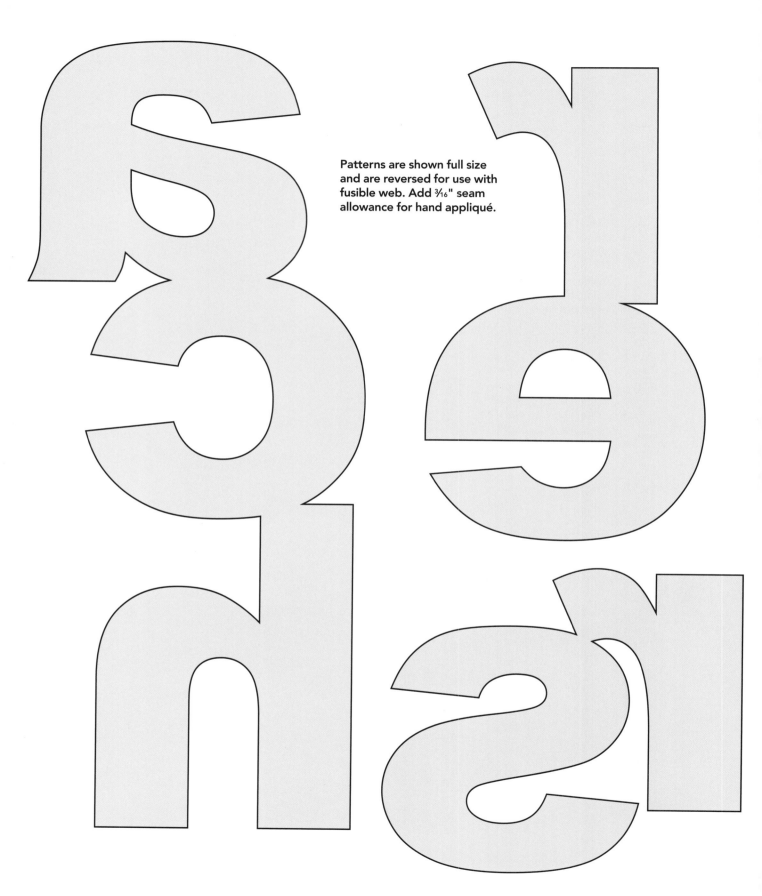

Patterns are shown full size and are reversed for use with fusible web. Add $\frac{3}{16}$" seam allowance for hand appliqué.

Patterns are shown full size and are reversed for use with fusible web. Add ³⁄₁₆" seam allowance for hand appliqué.

Scatter colorful signs of the season across a whimsical tablescape.

BUBBLY BUTTERFLIES
table runner + placemat

Table Runner Size: 14" × 40"

MATERIALS

⅝ yard kiwi print for background and binding

¼ yard lime print for border

1 fat quarter* lemon print for flower centers and corners

1 fat quarter* grape print for butterfly wings

1 fat eighth** boysenberry print for butterfly bodies

3 fat eighths** in orange, blue, and fuchsia prints for flowers

Paper-backed fusible web

Lavender embroidery thread

½ yard backing fabric

18" × 44" piece of quilt batting

*fat quarter = 18" × 20"

**fat eighth = 9" × 20"

Cutting for Table Runner

Measurements include ¼" seam allowances. Border strips are exact length needed. You may want to make them longer to allow for piecing variations. Follow manufacturer's instructions for using fusible web.

FROM KIWI PRINT, CUT:

- 1 (10½" × 36½") rectangle.
- 4 (2¼"-wide) strips for binding.

FROM LIME PRINT, CUT:

- 3 (2½"-wide) strips. From strips, cut 2 (2½" × 36½") side borders and 2 (2½" × 10½") top and bottom borders.

FROM LEMON PRINT, CUT:

- 1 (2½"-wide) strip. From strip, cut 4 (2½") squares.
- 2 Large Flower Centers.
- 2 Medium Flower Centers.
- 3 Small Flower Centers.

FROM GRAPE PRINT, CUT:

- 2 Large Butterfly Wings.
- 2 Small Butterfly Wings.

FROM BOYSENBERRY PRINT, CUT:

- 2 Large Butterfly Bodies.
- 2 Small Butterfly Bodies.

FROM ORANGE PRINT, CUT:

- 2 Large Flowers.

FROM BLUE PRINT, CUT:

- 2 Medium Flowers.

FROM FUCHSIA PRINT, CUT:

- 3 Small Flowers.

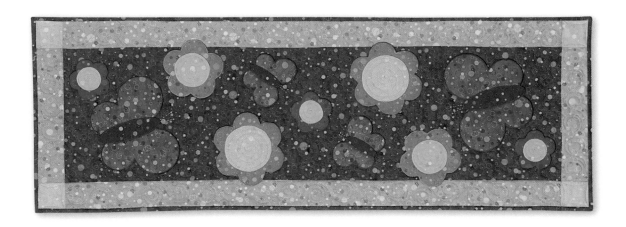

Table Runner Assembly

1 Add lime print side borders to kiwi print rectangle.

2 Add 1 lemon print square to each end of lime print top and bottom borders. Add borders to quilt.

3 Referring to Table Runner Diagrams and photo, position appliqué pieces atop quilt top; fuse in place.

4 Machine appliqué in place using satin stitch and matching thread.

Sew Smart™

Use tear-away stabilizer under your work to stabilize block when doing machine satin stitching. —Patrick

5 Using lavender embroidery thread, stitch antennae with running stitch (Running Stitch Diagram). Make a French Knot at end of each antenna (French Knot Diagram).

Running Stitch Diagram

French Knot Diagram

Finishing

1 Layer backing, batting, and quilt top; baste. Quilt as desired.

2 Join 2¼"-wide dark green strips into 1 continuous piece for straight-grain French-fold binding. Add binding to quilt.

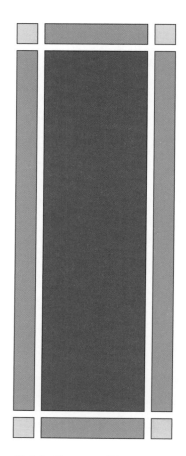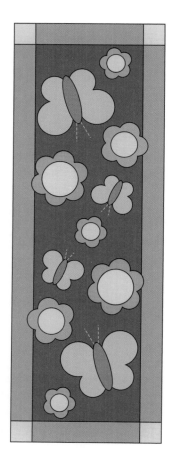

Table Runner Diagrams

Placemat Size: 15" diameter

PLACEMAT MATERIALS

½ yard kiwi print for mat and backing

1 fat quarter* lime print for binding

10" square lemon print for flower center

14" square blue print for flower

5" square grape print for butterfly wings

3" square boysenberry print for butterfly body

Paper-backed fusible web

Purple embroidery thread

18" square of quilt batting

*fat quarter = 18" × 20"

Cutting for Placemat

Measurements include ¼" seam allowances. Follow manufacturer's instructions for using fusible web.

FROM KIWI PRINT, CUT:

- 1 (18") square for backing.
- 1 Circle for background.

FROM LIME PRINT, CUT:

- 60" of 2¼"-wide bias strips. Join strips to make bias binding.

FROM LEMON PRINT, CUT:

- 1 Giant Flower Center.

FROM BLUE PRINT, CUT:

- 1 Giant Flower.

FROM GRAPE PRINT, CUT:

- 1 Small Butterfly Wings.

FROM BOYSENBERRY PRINT, CUT:

- 1 Small Butterfly Body.

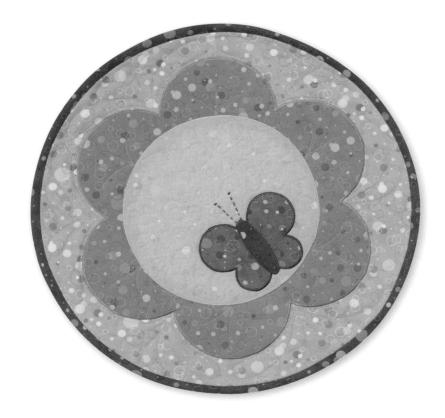

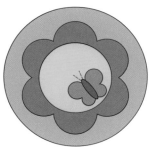

Appliqué Diagram

Mat Assembly

1 Position appliqué pieces on kiwi print background circle as shown in Appliqué Diagram and photo.

2 Fuse pieces in place. Machine appliqué using satin stitch and matching thread.

3 Using purple embroidery thread, stitch antennae with running stitch. Make a French Knot at end of each antenna.

Finishing

1 Layer backing, batting, and quilt top; baste. Quilt as desired.

2 Add binding to mat.

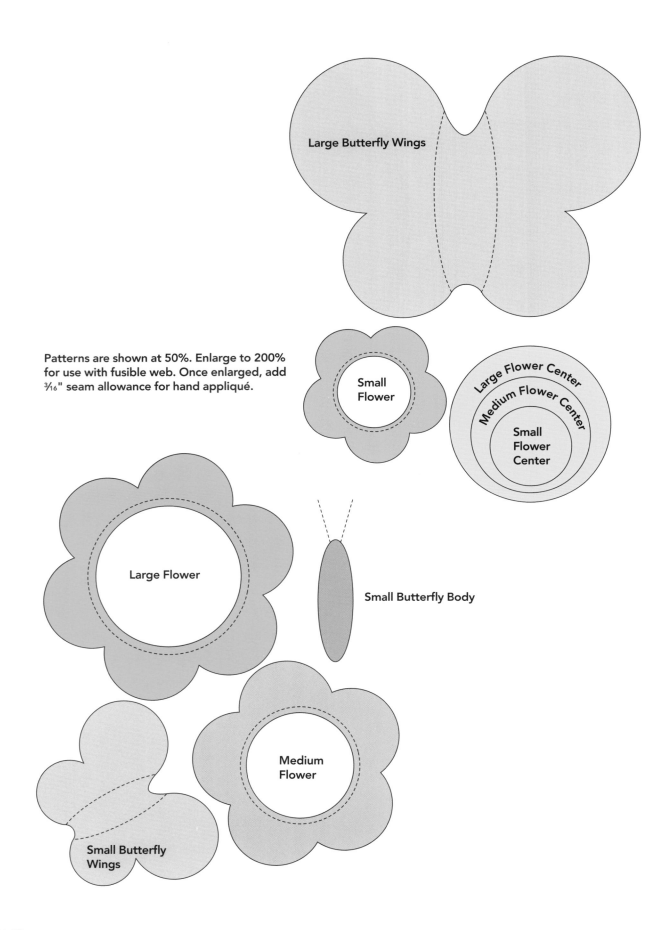

Large Butterfly Wings

Patterns are shown at 50%. Enlarge to 200% for use with fusible web. Once enlarged, add ³⁄₁₆" seam allowance for hand appliqué.

Small Flower

Large Flower Center

Medium Flower Center

Small Flower Center

Large Flower

Small Butterfly Body

Medium Flower

Small Butterfly Wings

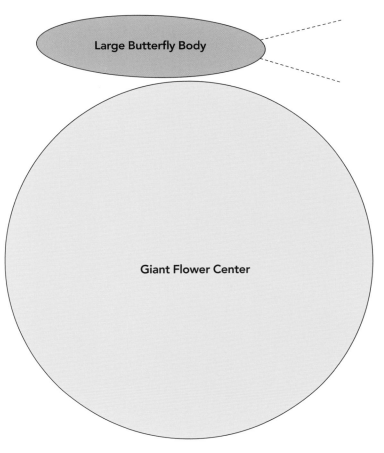

Large Butterfly Body

Giant Flower Center

Patterns are shown at 50%. Enlarge to 200% for use with fusible web. Once enlarged, add ³⁄₁₆" seam allowance for hand appliqué.

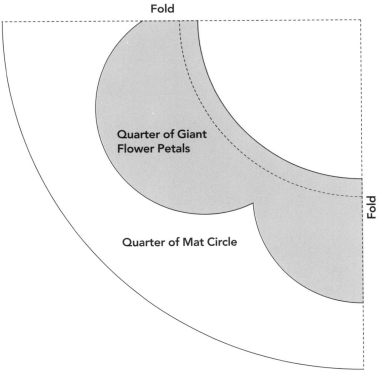

Fold

Quarter of Giant Flower Petals

Quarter of Mat Circle

Fold

Whimsical style shines through in this sunny wall hanging. It would aslo work well as a table runner.

SUNNY TRIO *wall hanging*

Size: 12" x 32"
Blocks: 3 (8") blocks

MATERIALS

½ yard turquoise print for blocks and binding

¼ yard purple print for sashing and border

1 fat quarter* gold print for blocks

1 fat eighth** brown print for blocks

1 fat quarter* green print for blocks

Paper-backed fusible web

½ yard backing fabric

Craft-size quilt batting

*fat quarter = 18" × 20"

**fat eighth = 9" × 20"

Sew Smart™

Work on an appliqué pressing sheet when fusing so you don't get fusible residue on your ironing surface.—Patrick

Cutting

Measurements include ¼" seam allowances. Border strips are exact length needed. You may want to make them longer to allow for piecing variations. Follow manufacturer's instructions for using fusible web.

FROM TURQUOISE PRINT, CUT:

- 1 (8½"-wide) strip. From strip, cut 3 (8½") squares.
- 3 (2¼"-wide) strips for binding.

FROM PURPLE PRINT, CUT:

- 3 (2½"-wide) strips. From strips, cut 2 (2½" x 32½") side borders and 4 (2½" x 8½") sashing rectangles.

FROM GOLD PRINT, CUT:

- 3 Flowers.

FROM BROWN PRINT, CUT:

- 3 Flower Centers.

FROM GREEN PRINT, CUT:

- 9 Leaves.

Block Assembly

1 Referring to Block Diagram, arrange 1 Flower, 1 Flower Center, and 3 Leaves on 1 turquoise background square as shown. Trim excess leaves under flower and even with edges of background square. Fuse pieces in place.

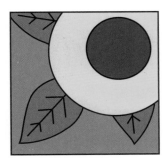

Block Diagram

2 Machine appliqué using matching thread and satin stitch. Satin stitch leaf veins as shown to complete 1 block (Block Diagram). Make 3 blocks.

Quilt Assembly

1 Lay out blocks and purple print sashing rectangles as shown in Quilt Top Assembly Diagram. Join to complete quilt center.

2 Add purple print side borders to quilt center.

Finishing

1 Layer backing, batting, and quilt top; baste. Quilt as desired. Quilt shown was echo quilted in blocks and with wavy parallel lines in sashing and borders (Quilting Diagram). The quilting thread colors match the fabrics.

2 Join 2¼"-wide turquoise print strips into 1 continuous piece for straight-grain French-fold binding. Add binding to quilt.

Quilt Top Assembly Diagram

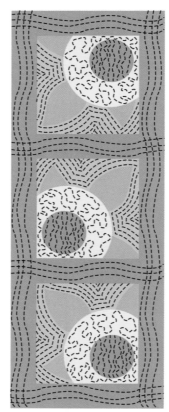

Quilting Diagram

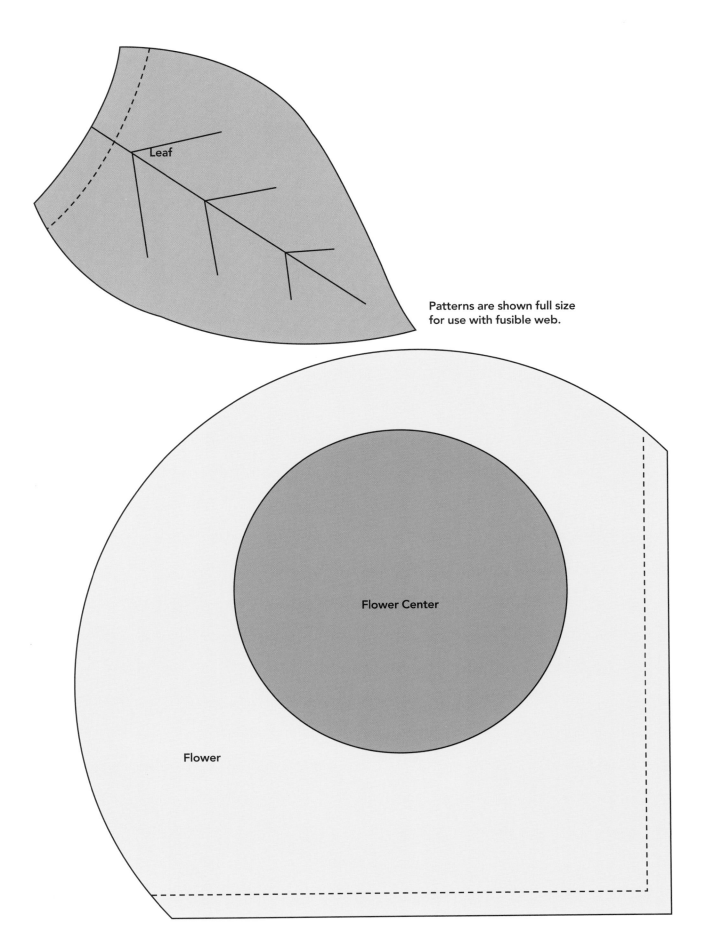

Leaf

Patterns are shown full size
for use with fusible web.

Flower Center

Flower

This watchful, wide-eyed owl wall hanging is the perfect piece to spruce up a small space.

NIGHT OWL *wall hanging*

Size: 12" × 18"

MATERIALS

1 fat quarter* blue print

1 fat quarter* green print

5" × 12" rectangle dark brown print

10" square medium brown print

10" square light brown print

10" square white print

8" square orange print

6" square black print

6" square gold print

4" square dark gold print

Paper-backed fusible web

1 fat quarter* backing fabric

16" × 20" piece of quilt batting

*fat quarter = 18" × 20"

Cutting

Measurements include ¼" seam allowances. Follow manufacturer's instructions for using fusible web.

FROM BLUE PRINT, CUT:

- 1 (12½" × 18½") rectangle.

FROM GREEN PRINT, CUT:

- 4 (2¼"-wide) strips for binding.
- 1 Large Leaf.
- 2 Medium Leaves.
- 2 Small Leaves.

FROM DARK BROWN PRINT, CUT:

- 1 Branch.

FROM MEDIUM BROWN PRINT, CUT:

- 1 Owl Body.

FROM LIGHT BROWN PRINT, CUT:

- 1 Owl Wing.
- 1 Owl Wing reversed.
- 1 Owl Brow.

FROM WHITE PRINT, CUT:

- 1 Moon.
- 1 Outer Eye Unit.
- 2 Eye Highlights.

FROM ORANGE PRINT, CUT:

- 2 Middle Eyes.

FROM BLACK PRINT, CUT:

- 2 Inner Eyes.

FROM GOLD PRINT, CUT:

- 3 Stars.

FROM DARK GOLD PRINT, CUT:

- 1 Beak.

Web Extra

Machine embroidery appliqué design is available for this project. For ordering information, go to www.Quilting Celebrations.com/embroidery.

Assembly

1 Position appliqué pieces atop blue print background rectangle as shown in photo; fuse in place.

2 Machine appliqué using satin stitch and matching thread.

Finishing

1 Layer backing, batting, and quilt top; baste. Quilt as desired.

2 Join 2¼"-wide green strips into 1 continuous piece for straight-grain French-fold binding. Add binding to quilt.

Sew Smart™

Work on an appliqué pressing sheet so you don't get fusible residue on your ironing surface. —Patrick

Sew Smart™

Use tear-away stabilizer under your work to stabilize the wall hanging when doing machine satin stitching.—Patrick

Sew Smart™

Add a sleeve to the back of the quilt for easy hanging. Refer to the Techniques section for instructions.—Patrick

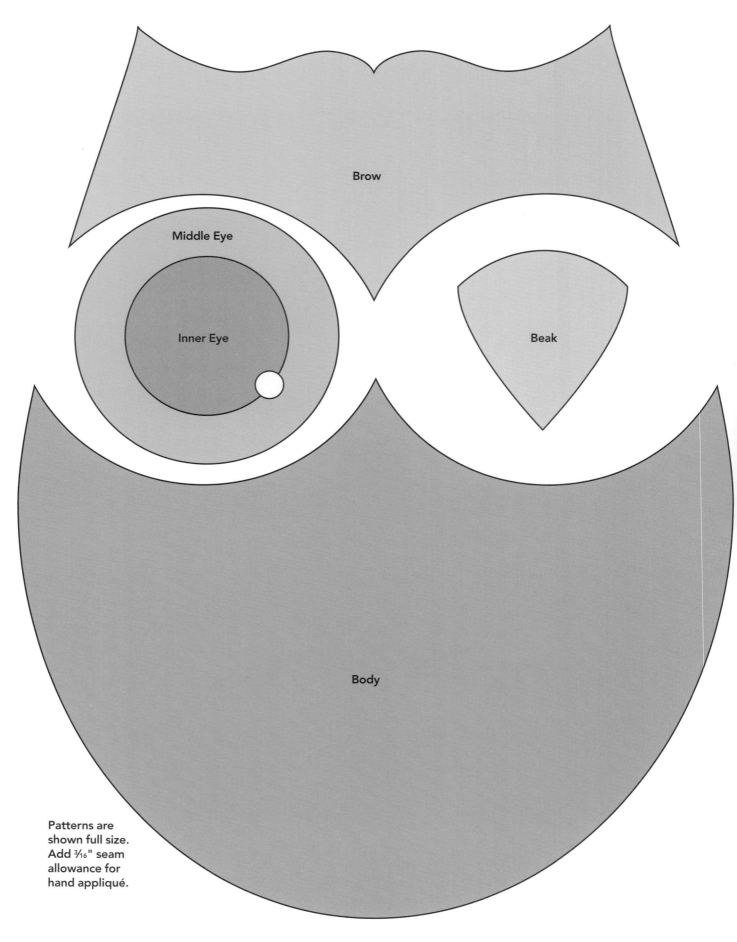

Brow

Middle Eye

Inner Eye

Beak

Body

Patterns are
shown full size.
Add ³⁄₁₆" seam
allowance for
hand appliqué.

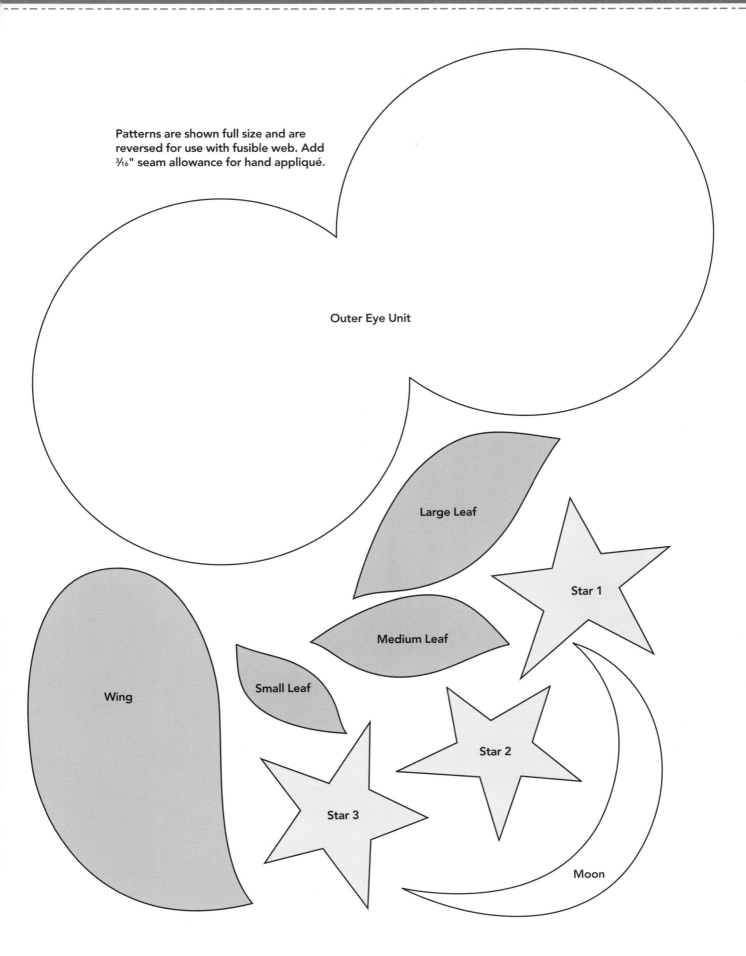

Patterns are shown full size and are reversed for use with fusible web. Add ³⁄₁₆" seam allowance for hand appliqué.

Outer Eye Unit

Large Leaf

Star 1

Medium Leaf

Wing

Small Leaf

Star 2

Star 3

Moon

Wrap this cozy quilt around you as you hunt for falling stars on summer nights. The simple design lends itself to endless color combinations; create one for every season!

FALLING STARS *quilt*

Size: 48" × 57"

MATERIALS

½ yard yellow print

⅝ yard orange print

⅝ yard green print

⅝ yard purple print

⅝ yard black print

1½ yards white-on-white print

Paper-backed fusible web

3 yards backing fabric

Twin-size quilt batting

Web Extra

Machine embroidery appliqué design is available for this project. For ordering information, go to www.Quilting Celebrations.com/embroidery.

Cutting

Measurements include ¼" seam allowances. Follow manufacturer's instructions for using fusible web.

FROM YELLOW PRINT, CUT:

- 2 (3½"-wide) strips for strip sets.
- 1 (2½"-wide) strip. From strip, cut 2 (2½" × 15½") rectangles.
- 2 Large Inner Stars.

FROM ORANGE PRINT, CUT:

- 2 (3½"-wide) strips for strip sets.
- 2 (2½"-wide) strips. From strips, cut 4 (2½" × 15½") rectangles.
- 2 Small Inner Stars.

FROM GREEN PRINT, CUT:

- 2 (3½"-wide) strips for strip sets.
- 2 (2½"-wide) strips. From strips, cut 4 (2½" × 15½") rectangles.
- 1 Large Inner Star.
- 1 Small Inner Star.

FROM PURPLE PRINT, CUT:

- 2 (3½"-wide) strips for strip sets.
- 2 (2½"-wide) strips. From strips, cut 4 (2½" × 15½") rectangles.
- 1 Small Inner Star.

FROM BLACK PRINT, CUT:

- 4 (2½"-wide) strips. From strips, cut 7 (2½" × 15½") rectangles.
- 3 Large Stars.
- 4 Small Stars.

FROM REMAINDERS OF YELLOW, ORANGE, GREEN, PURPLE, AND BLACK PRINTS, CUT A TOTAL OF :

- 7 (2¼"-wide) strips. Cut strips into various lengths from 18" to 40". Join strips for binding.

FROM WHITE-ON-WHITE PRINT, CUT:

- 11 (3½"-wide) lengthwise strips. From strips, cut 6 (3½" × 51½") vertical sashing strips and side borders, 2 (3½" × 48½") top and bottom borders, and 18 (3½" × 6½") horizontal sashing strips.

Block Assembly

1 Join 1 black print rectangle and 2 purple print rectangles as shown in Rectangular Block Diagrams. Make 2 purple, 1 yellow, 2 green, and 2 orange rectangular blocks.

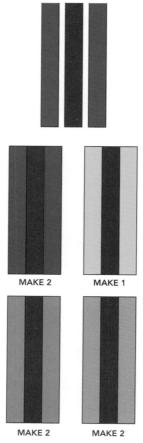

MAKE 2 MAKE 1

MAKE 2 MAKE 2

Rectangular Block Diagrams

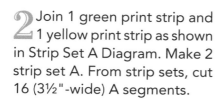

Sew Smart™

Stitch your blocks "assembly-line style" to save time. —Patrick

2 Join 1 green print strip and 1 yellow print strip as shown in Strip Set A Diagram. Make 2 strip set A. From strip sets, cut 16 (3½"-wide) A segments.

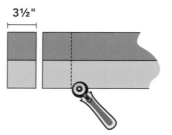

3½"

Strip Set A Diagram

3 Join 1 purple print strip and 1 orange print strip as shown in Strip Set B Diagram. Make 2 strip set B. From strip sets, cut 16 (3½"-wide) B segments.

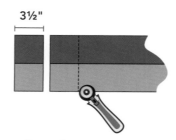

3½"

Strip Set B Diagram

4 Join 1 segment A and 1 segment B as shown in Four Patch Block Diagrams. Make 16 Four Patch blocks.

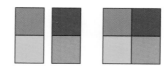

Four Patch Block Diagrams

Quilt Assembly

1 Lay out blocks, horizontal sashing strips, and vertical sashing strips as shown in Quilt Top Assembly Diagram.

2 Join blocks and horizontal sashing strips into vertical rows. Join rows and vertical sashing strips to complete quilt center.

3 Add side borders to quilt center. Add top and bottom borders to quilt.

4 Referring to photo on page 69, position stars atop quilt top; fuse in place. Machine appliqué using black thread and satin stitch.

Finishing

1 Divide backing into 2 (1½-yard) lengths. Cut 1 piece in half lengthwise to make 2 narrow panels. Join 1 narrow panel to wider panel. Seam will run horizontally. Remaining panel is extra and can be used to make a hanging sleeve.

2 Layer backing, batting, and quilt top; baste. Quilt as desired.

3 Add binding to quilt.

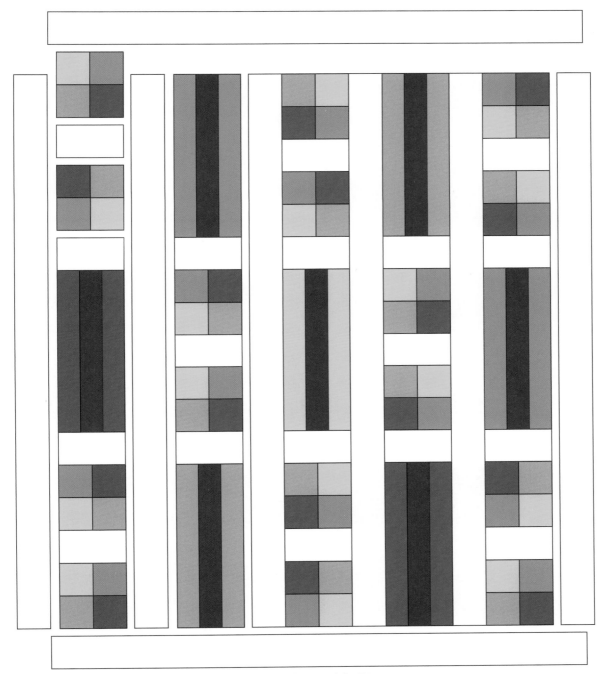

Quilt Top Assembly Diagram

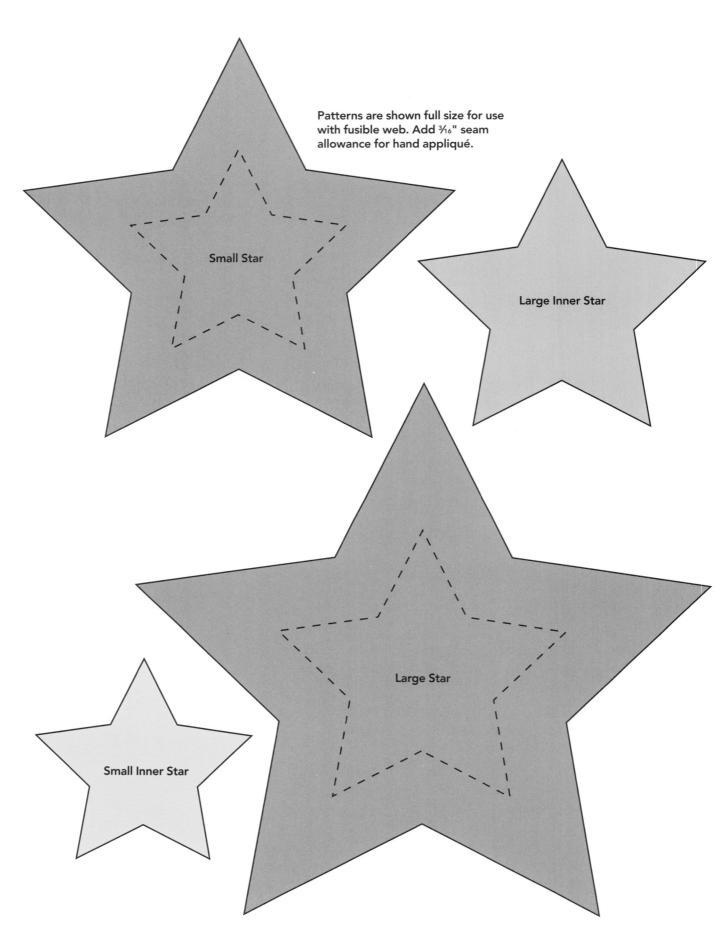

Patterns are shown full size for use with fusible web. Add ³⁄₁₆" seam allowance for hand appliqué.

Small Star

Large Inner Star

Large Star

Small Inner Star

Using metallic thread for the quilting and satin stitching on this dynamic duo will put the "pop" in your patriotic party.

FIRECRACKERS FOR THE FOURTH

FIRECRACKERS FOR THE FOURTH

Banner

Size: 13" × 30"

MATERIALS

⅝ yard navy print for background and binding

1 fat quarter* cardinal print

1 fat quarter* ivory print

Paper-backed fusible web

½ yard backing fabric

17" × 34" piece of quilt batting

*fat quarter = 18" × 20"

Cutting

Measurements include ¼" seam allowances. Follow manufacturer's instructions for using fusible web.

FROM NAVY PRINT, CUT:

- 1 (13½"-wide) strip. From strip, cut 1 (13½" × 16½") A rectangle and 2 (13½" × 3½") B rectangles.

- 3 (2¼"-wide) strips for binding.

FROM CARDINAL PRINT, CUT:

- 5 (1½"-wide) strips. From strips, cut 2 (1½" × 13½") C rectangles and 14 (1½" × 3½") D rectangles.

- 3 Firecrackers.

FROM IVORY PRINT, CUT:

- 3 (1½"-wide) strips. From strips, cut 12 (1½" × 3½") D rectangles.

- 6 Large Stars.

- 3 Firecracker Sparkles.

- 1 "4."

- 2 H.

- 1 A.

- 2 P.

- 1 Y.

- 1 T.

Banner Assembly

1 Join navy print rectangles and cardinal print C rectangles as shown in Quilt Top Assembly Diagram.

2 Position appliqué pieces atop pieced center rectangle; fuse in place.

Sew Smart™

This project is a perfect for raw-edge appliqué, but if you'll be washing it, you'll want to satin-stitch the edges. —Patrick

3 Join 7 cardinal print D rectangles and 6 ivory print D rectangles to make pieced top border. Repeat for pieced bottom border.

4 Add pieced top and bottom borders to quilt.

Finishing

1 Layer backing, batting, and quilt top; baste. Quilt as desired.

2 Join 2¼"-wide navy print strips into 1 continuous piece for straight-grain French-fold binding. Add binding to quilt.

Sew Smart™

Add a sleeve to the back of banner for easy hanging. Refer to the Techniques section at the end of the book for instructions.—Patrick

Quilt Top Assembly Diagram

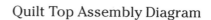

FIRECRACKERS FOR THE FOURTH
Table Topper

Size: 20" diameter

MATERIALS

⅝ yard navy print

1 fat quarter* cardinal print

1 fat eighth** ivory print

Paper-backed fusible web

Gold metallic thread for machine appliqué

⅝ yard backing fabric

24" square quilt batting

*fat quarter = 18" × 20"

**fat eighth = 9" × 20"

Cutting

Measurements include ¼" seam allowances. Pattern for background is on page 19. Follow manufacturer's instructions for using fusible web.

FROM NAVY PRINT, CUT:

• 1 Table Topper Background.

FROM CARDINAL PRINT, CUT:

• 4 Firecrackers.

• 80" of 2¼"-wide bias strips. Join strips to make bias binding.

FROM IVORY PRINT, CUT:

• 4 Large Stars.

• 4 Small Stars.

• 4 Firecracker Sparkles.

Table Topper Assembly

1 Referring to the photo above, arrange appliqué pieces atop navy print background; fuse pieces in place.

2 Machine appliqué using satin stitch and gold metallic thread. Stitch dynamite detail and fuses with satin stitch and gold thread.

Sew Smart™

Use tear-away stabilizer under your work to stabilize centerpiece when doing machine satin stitching.—Patrick

Finishing

1 Layer backing, batting, and quilt top; baste. Quilt as desired.

2 Add binding to quilt.

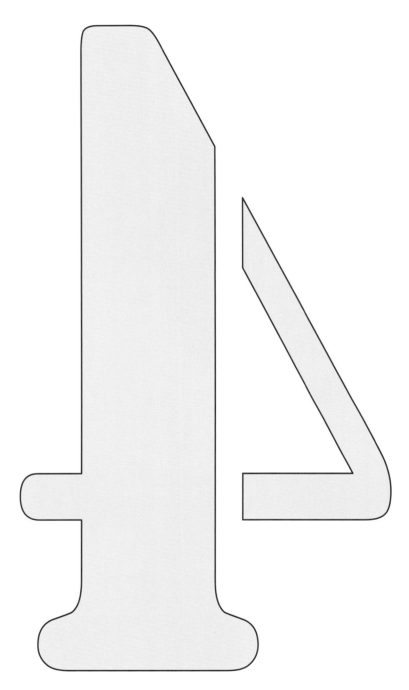

Patterns are shown full size
and are reversed for use with
fusible web. Add ³⁄₁₆" seam
allowance for hand appliqué.

Stars

Firecracker
Sparkle

Patterns are shown full size
and are reversed for use with
fusible web. Add ³⁄₁₆" seam
allowance for hand appliqué.

Firecracker

Mat Assembly

1 Referring to photo, position appliqué pieces atop navy print background square; fuse in place.

Sew Smart™

Work on an appliqué pressing sheet so you don't get fusible residue on your ironing surface.—Patrick

2 Trim petals and centers even with edges of background square.

Finishing

1 Layer backing, batting, and quilt top; baste.

2 Stitching through all layers, machine appliqué shapes using satin stitch and matching thread.

3 Stitch veins on leaves and petals using satin stitch and matching thread.

4 Join 2¼"-wide cocoa print strips into 1 continuous piece for straight-grain French-fold binding. Add binding to quilt.

Sew Smart™

Add a sleeve to the back of banner for easy hanging. Refer to the Techniques section at the end of the book for instructions.—Patrick

STYLISH SUNFLOWERS
mini mat

Size: 12" × 12"

MATERIALS

1 fat quarter* navy print

1 fat quarter* cocoa print

1 fat eighth** yellow print

1 fat eighth** gold print

8" square celery print

1 fat quarter* backing fabric

16" square quilt batting

*fat quarter = 18" × 20"

**fat eighth = 9" × 20"

Cutting

Measurements include ¼" seam allowances. Follow manufacturer's instructions for using fusible web.

FROM NAVY PRINT FAT QUARTER, CUT:

• 1 (12½") square.

FROM COCOA PRINT FAT QUARTER, CUT:

• 3 (2¼"-wide) strips for binding.

• 2 Centers.

FROM YELLOW PRINT FAT EIGHTH, CUT:

• 2 Petal Units.

FROM GOLD PRINT FAT EIGHTH, CUT:

• 2 Petal Units.

FROM CELERY PRINT, CUT:

• 1 Upper Leaf.

• 1 Lower Leaf.

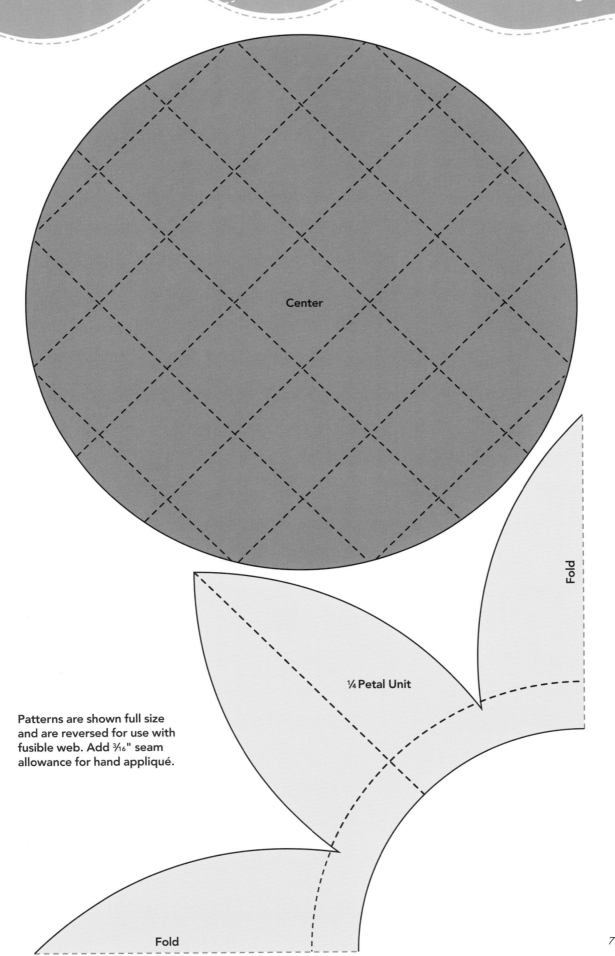

Center

Fold

¼ Petal Unit

Patterns are shown full size
and are reversed for use with
fusible web. Add ³⁄₁₆" seam
allowance for hand appliqué.

Fold

These brightly colored garden dwellers are really quite friendly! Small children can have fun counting ladybugs, spots, and squares.

SEEING SPOTS *quilt*

Size: 40" × 40"
Blocks: 16 (6") blocks

MATERIALS

1 yard snow print for sashing and outer border

⅞ yard lime print for blocks and binding

⅝ yard blue print for blocks and inner border

4 fat quarters* in raspberry, bubblegum, apricot, and orange prints for ladybugs and sashing squares

Paper-backed fusible web

2¾ yards backing fabric

Crib-size quilt batting

*fat quarter = 18" × 20"

Cutting

Measurements include ¼" seam allowances. Border strips are exact length needed. You may want to make them longer to allow for piecing variations. Follow manufacturer's instructions for using fusible web.

FROM SNOW PRINT, CUT:

- 11 (2½"-wide) strips. From strips, cut 2 (2½" × 36½") side outer borders, 2 (2½" × 40½") top and bottom outer borders, and 40 (2½" × 6½") C rectangles.

FROM LIME PRINT, CUT:

- 2 (6½"-wide) strips. From strips, cut 8 (6½") A squares.

- 5 (2¼"-wide) strips for binding.

FROM BLUE PRINT, CUT:

- 2 (6½"-wide) strips. From strips, cut 8 (6½") A squares.

- 4 (1½"-wide) strips. From strips, cut 2 (1½" × 34½") side inner borders, 2 (1½" × 36½") top and bottom inner borders.

FROM RASPBERRY PRINT FAT QUARTER, CUT:

- 8 Ladybug Bodies.

FROM BUBBLEGUM PRINT FAT QUARTER, CUT:

- 2 (2½"-wide) strips. From strips, cut 12 (2½") B squares.

- 8 Heads.

- 8 sets of Spots.

FROM APRICOT PRINT FAT QUARTER, CUT:

- 8 Ladybug Bodies.

FROM ORANGE PRINT FAT QUARTER, CUT:

- 2 (2½"-wide) strips. From strips, cut 13 (2½") B squares.

- 8 Heads.

- 8 sets of Spots.

Block Assembly

1 Referring to photo on page 80, position 1 raspberry print Ladybug Body, 1 bubblegum print Head, and 1 set of bubblegum print Spots atop 1 lime print A square; fuse in place.

2 Machine appliqué in place using satin stitch and matching thread. Stitch antennae with satin stitch and matching thread.

Sew Smart™

Use tear-away stabilizer under your work to stabilize block when doing machine satin stitching. —Patrick

3 Make 8 blocks with raspberry print ladybugs on lime print background and 8 blocks with apricot print ladybugs on blue print background (Block Diagrams).

MAKE 8   MAKE 8

Block Diagrams

Quilt Assembly

1 Lay out blocks, snow print C rectangles, and orange print and bubblegum print B squares as shown in Quilt Top Assembly Diagram.

2 Join into rows; join rows to complete quilt center.

3 Add blue print side inner borders to quilt center. Add blue print top and bottom inner borders to quilt.

4 Repeat for snow print outer borders.

Finishing

1 Divide backing into 2 (1⅜-yard) lengths. Cut 1 piece in half lengthwise to make 2 narrow panels. Join 1 narrow panel to wider panel. Remaining panel is extra and can be used to make a hanging sleeve.

Sew Smart™

Add a sleeve to the back of banner for easy hanging. Refer to the Techniques section at the end of the book for instructions.—Patrick

2 Layer backing, batting, and quilt top; baste. Quilt as desired.

3 Join 2¼"-wide lime print strips into 1 continuous piece for straight-grain French-fold binding. Add binding to quilt.

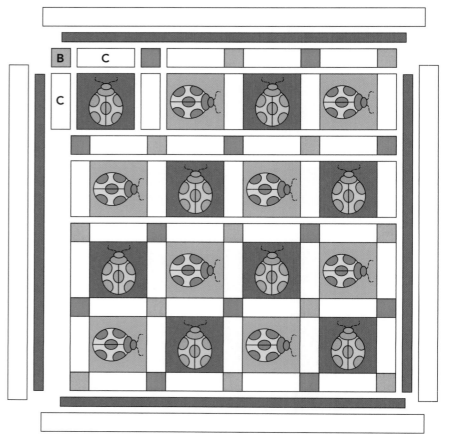

Quilt Top Assembly Diagram

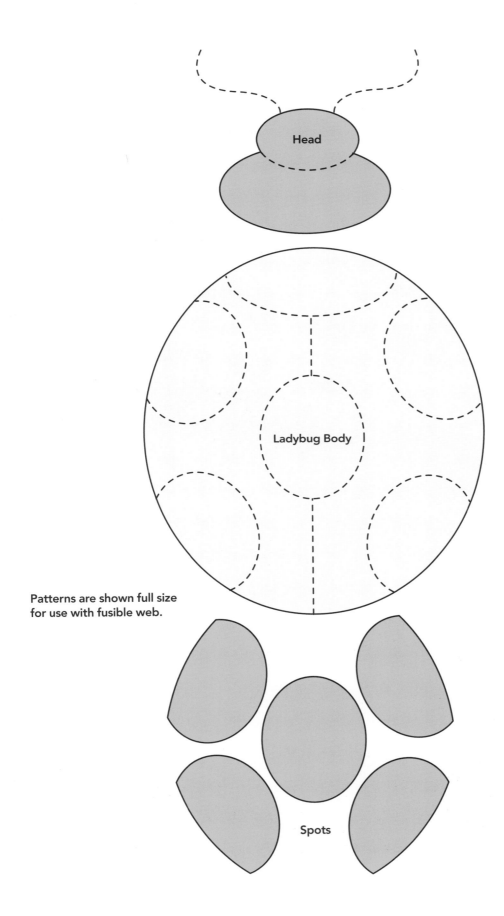

Head

Ladybug Body

Patterns are shown full size
for use with fusible web.

Spots

Simple to piece and appliqué, these placemats and coordinating mug mats are also great stash busters.

ACORN &
OAK LEAVES

ACORN & OAK LEAVES
placemats

Size: 14" × 18"

MATERIALS

NOTE: MATERIALS LISTED ARE FOR 2 PLACEMATS.

½ yard green print

⅜ yard dark brown print

1 fat quarter* brown print

1 fat quarter* rust print

1 fat quarter * orange print

Paper-backed fusible web

½ yard backing piece

2 (16" × 20") pieces of quilt batting

*fat quarter = 18" × 20"

Web Extra

Machine embroidery appliqué design is available for this project. For ordering information, go to www.QuiltingCelebrations. com/embroidery.

Cutting

Measurements include ¼" seam allowances. Follow manufacturer's instructions for using fusible web.

FROM GREEN PRINT, CUT:

• 1 (14½" × 12½) A rectangle.

FROM DARK BROWN PRINT, CUT:

• 2 (2¼"-wide) strips for binding.

• 1 Acorn Cap.

• 1 Acorn Stem.

FROM BROWN PRINT, CUT:

• 2 (2½"-wide) strips. From strips, cut 8 (2½") B squares.

• 1 Acorn.

FROM RUST PRINT, CUT:

• 1 (2½"-wide) strip. From strip, cut 3 (2½") B squares.

• 1 leaf.

FROM ORANGE PRINT, CUT:

• 2 (2½"-wide) strips. From strips, cut 10 (2½") B squares.

• 1 leaf.

Mat Assembly

1 Lay out B squares as shown in Background Assembly Diagrams on following page. Join squares into rows; join rows to make Side Unit.

2 Add Side Unit to green print A rectangle as shown.

3 Arrange appliqué pieces on background as shown in photo; fuse in place.

4 Machine appliqué using satin stitch and matching thread. Stitch leaf veins and acorn details.

Sew Smart™

Pull the tail end of your thread in front of the needle and stitch over it when beginning a new line of satin stitching. This eliminates a loose end that can come unstitched.—Patrick

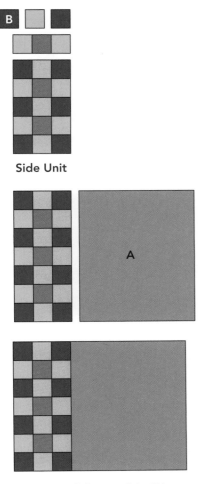

Side Unit

A

Background Assembly Diagrams

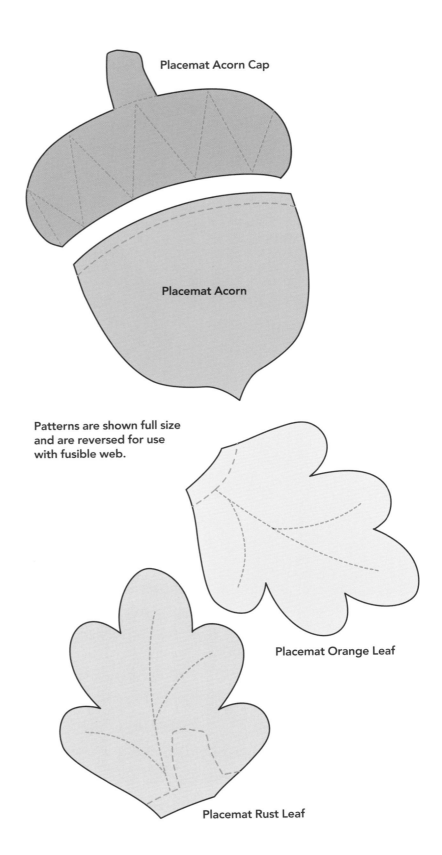

Placemat Acorn Cap

Placemat Acorn

Patterns are shown full size
and are reversed for use
with fusible web.

Placemat Orange Leaf

Placemat Rust Leaf

Finishing

1 Layer backing, batting, and quilt top base; baste. Quilt as desired.

2 Join 2¼"-wide dark brown strips into 1 continuous piece for straight-grain French-fold binding. Add binding to placemat.

ACORN & OAK LEAVES
mug mats

Size: 7½" diameter

MATERIALS

NOTE: MATERIALS LISTED ARE FOR 2 MUG MATS.

½ yard green print

⅜ yard dark brown print

8" square brown print

8" square rust print

8" square orange print

Paper-backed fusible web

2 (10") squares of quilt batting

*fat quarter = 18" × 20"

Web Extra

Machine embroidery appliqué design is available for this project. For ordering information, go to www.QuiltingCelebrations.com/embroidery.

Cutting

Measurements include ¼" seam allowances. Follow manufacturer's instructions for using fusible web.

FROM GREEN PRINT, CUT:

• 1 Mug Mat background.

• 1 (10") square for backing.

FROM DARK BROWN PRINT, CUT:

• 30" of 2¼"-wide bias strips. Join strips to make bias binding.

• 1 Acorn Cap.

FROM BROWN PRINT, CUT:

• 1 Acorn.

FROM RUST PRINT, CUT:

• 1 Leaf.

FROM ORANGE PRINT, CUT:

• 1 Leaf.

Mat Assembly

1 Position appliqué pieces on green print circle as shown in photo.

2 Fuse pieces in place.

Finishing

1 Layer backing, batting, and quilt top; baste. Quilt as desired.

2 Stitching through all layers, machine appliqué using satin stitch and matching thread. Stitch leaf veins and acorn details.

3 Trim backing and batting even with edges of background.

4 Add binding to mat.

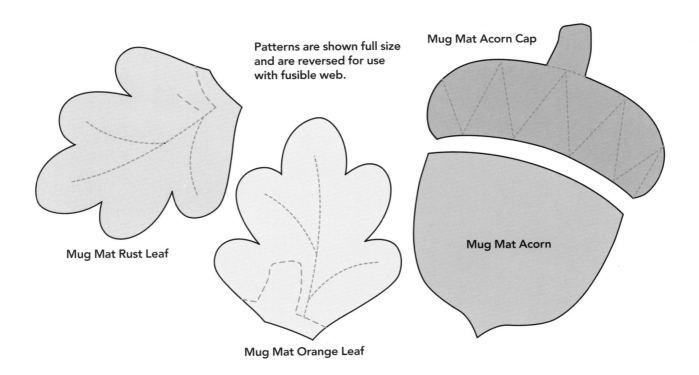

Patterns are shown full size and are reversed for use with fusible web.

Mug Mat Acorn Cap

Mug Mat Rust Leaf

Mug Mat Acorn

Mug Mat Orange Leaf

Mug Mat Background

Pattern is shown at 50%. Enlarge to 200% before using.

Rustic yarn-dyed plaids and earthy tone-on-tone prints are the perfect background for this ornamental acorn.

MIGHTY ACORN *pillow*

Size: 14" × 14"

MATERIALS

1 fat eighth* tan plaid

⅜ yard brown plaid for outer border and backing

1 fat quarter** tan print

1 fat quarter** brown print

Paper-backed fusible web

1 yard lining fabric

Craft-size quilt batting

1⅝ yards brown pillow trim

14" square pillow form

*fat eighth = 9" × 20"

**fat quarter = 18" × 20"

Web Extra

Machine embroidery appliqué design is available for this project. For ordering information, go to www.QuiltingCelebrations.com/embroidery.

Cutting

Measurements include ¼" seam allowances. Follow manufacturer's instructions for using fusible web.

FROM TAN PLAID, CUT:

- 1 (6½") A square for center background.

FROM BROWN PLAID, CUT:

- 1 (9½"-wide) strip. From strip, cut 2 (9½" × 14½") backing rectangles.
- 2 (2½"-wide) strips. From strips, cut 2 (2½" × 14½") top and bottom outer borders and 2 (2½" × 10½") side outer borders.
- 1 (2¼"-wide) strip for binding.

FROM TAN PRINT, CUT:

- 2 (2½"-wide) strips. From strips, cut 8 (2½") B squares.
- 1 Acorn Cap.

FROM BROWN PRINT, CUT:

- 2 (2½"-wide) strips. From strips, cut 8 (2½") B squares.
- 1 Acorn.
- 1 Stem.

FROM LINING FABRIC, CUT:

- 1 (18"-wide) strip. From strip, cut 1 (18") front lining square.
- 2 (14"-wide) strips. From strips, cut 2 (14" × 18") back lining rectangles.

FROM BATTING, CUT:

- 2 (14" × 18") rectangles for back.
- 1 (18") square for front.

Pillow Top Assembly

1 Arrange appliqué pieces on A square as shown in photo and Pillow Top Diagrams; fuse in place.

2 Machine appliqué using satin stitch and matching thread.

Sew Smart™

If you are using the digitized embroidery file, follow instructions included for stitching order. —Patrick

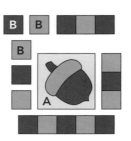

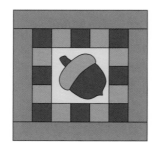

Pillow Top Diagrams

3 Join 2 tan print B squares and 1 brown print B square as shown to make 1 pieced side border. Make 2 pieced side borders. Add borders to center.

4 Join 3 brown print B squares and 2 tan print B squares as shown to make pieced top border. Add border to center. Repeat for pieced bottom border.

5 Add brown plaid side outer borders to center. Add brown plaid top and bottom outer borders to pillow top.

6 Layer lining square, batting square, and pillow top; baste. Quilt as desired.

7 Trim batting and lining even with edges of pillow top.

Finishing

1 Layer 1 lining rectangle, 1 batting rectangle, and 1 backing rectangle; baste. Quilt as desired.

2 Trim batting and lining even with edges of backing rectangle.

3 Add binding strip to 1 long edge of quilted back rectangle.

4 Make 2 back rectangles.

5 Overlap bound edges of back rectangles making back square the same size as pillow top. Baste overlapped edges together (Backing Diagram).

Backing Diagram

6 Baste trim to right side of pillow top, aligning edge of trim with edge of pillow top.

7 Place pillow top atop pillow back, right sides facing. Stitch around outer edge.

Sew Smart™

Take care to avoid catching the trim in the seam. I use a zipper foot for this step.—Patrick

8 Turn right side out through opening in pillow back. Insert pillow form into pillow cover.

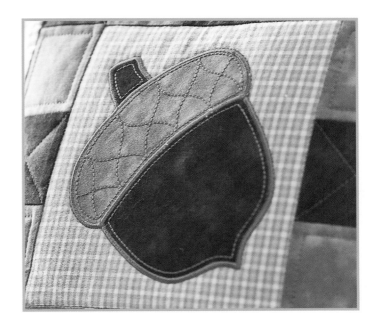

Patterns are shown full size and are reversed for use with fusible web. Add ³⁄₁₆" seam allowance for hand appliqué.

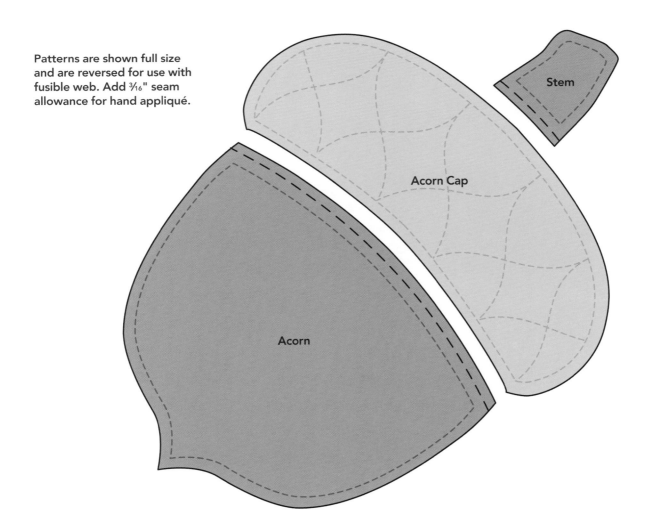

Stem

Acorn Cap

Acorn

The top layer of fine black tulle lends a foggy-night feel to this spooky scene.

SPOOKY SILHOUETTE *pennant*

Size: 12" × 18"

MATERIALS

1 fat quarter* dark orange print

10" square light orange print

¾ yard black print

Paper-backed fusible web

½ yard black tulle

1 fat quarter* backing fabric

14" × 20" piece of quilt batting

12"-wide wall or table hanger (optional)

*fat quarter = 18" × 20"

Cutting

Measurements include ¼" seam allowances. Follow manufacturer's instructions for using fusible web.

FROM DARK ORANGE PRINT, CUT:

* 1 (12" × 18") rectangle.

FROM LIGHT ORANGE PRINT, CUT:

* 1 Moon.

FROM BLACK PRINT, CUT:

* 64" of 2¼"-wide bias strips. Join strips to make bias binding.

* 1 Silhouette shape.

* 1 Small Bat.

* 1 Large Bat.

* 1 Half Circle.

FROM BLACK TULLE, CUT:

* 1 (12" × 18") rectangle.

Pennant Assembly

1 Trim end of dark orange print rectangle as shown in Background Trimming Diagram, using half circle template as a guide.

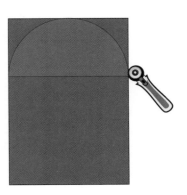

Background Trimming Diagram

2 Arrange appliqué pieces on background as shown in photo; fuse in place.

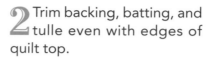

Sew Smart™

Work on an appliqué pressing sheet so you don't get fusible residue on your ironing surface.—Patrick

Finishing

1 Layer backing, batting, quilt top, and tulle; baste. Quilt as desired.

2 Trim backing, batting, and tulle even with edges of quilt top.

3 Hem straight edge of black print half circle. Baste half circle to back of quilt, aligning curved edges as shown in Back Diagram.

4 Add binding to quilt.

Back Diagram

Pattern is shown at 50%. Enlarge to 200% before using.

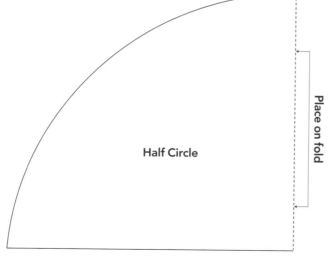

Half Circle

Place on fold

Pattern is shown at
50%. Enlarge to 200%
before using.

Spooky Silhouette

Bold letters and cheery colors exclaim a seasonal sentiment in this fabulous festoon.

HAPPY HAUNTING
pennant banner

MATERIALS

10 fat quarters* assorted prints in gold, orange, purple, and green

1 fat quarter* black print

2½ yards black pom-pom trim

2½ yards ⅞"-wide black ribbon

Paper-backed fusible web

Template material

*fat quarter = 18" × 20"

Cutting

Follow manufacturer's instructions for using fusible web.

Web Extra

Machine embroidery appliqué design is available for this project. For ordering information, go to www.QuiltingCelebrations.com/embroidery.

FROM ASSORTED PRINTS, CUT A TOTAL OF:

- 14 pairs of (7" x 9½") rectangles.

FROM BLACK PRINT, CUT:

- 2 Hs.
- 2 As.
- 2 Ps.
- 1 Y.
- 1 U.

- 2 Ns.
- 1 T.
- 1 I.
- 1 G.
- 1 Star.

FROM PAPER-BACKED FUSIBLE WEB, CUT:

- 14 (6½" x 9") rectangles.

Pennant Assembly

1 Position 1 letter on 1 print rectangle as shown in photo and Pennant Diagrams; fuse in place.

2 Machine appliqué using satin stitch and black thread.

3 Apply 1 fusible web rectangle to 1 matching print rectangle. Fuse rectangle to appliquéd rectangle to make double-sided fabric. NOTE: Center the fusible web rectangle between the fabric rectangles. The excess fabric will be trimmed off when cutting the pennant shape.

4 Cut pennant shape from double-sided fabric rectangle.

5 Top stitch ¼" from edge of sides and bottom of pennant.

6 Make remaining pennants in the same manner.

Finishing

1 Aligning top edges, join pom-pom trim and pennants.

2 Cut ribbon into 2 equal lengths. Fold each length in half. Attach ribbons to ends of pom-pom trim to complete pennant garland.

Pennant Diagrams

Patterns are shown full size and are reversed for use with fusible web. Add ³⁄₁₆" seam allowance for hand appliqué.

Patterns are shown full size and are reversed for use with fusible web. Add ³⁄₁₆" seam allowance for hand appliqué.

Patterns are shown full size and are
reversed for use with fusible web. Add
$\frac{3}{16}$" seam allowance for hand appliqué.

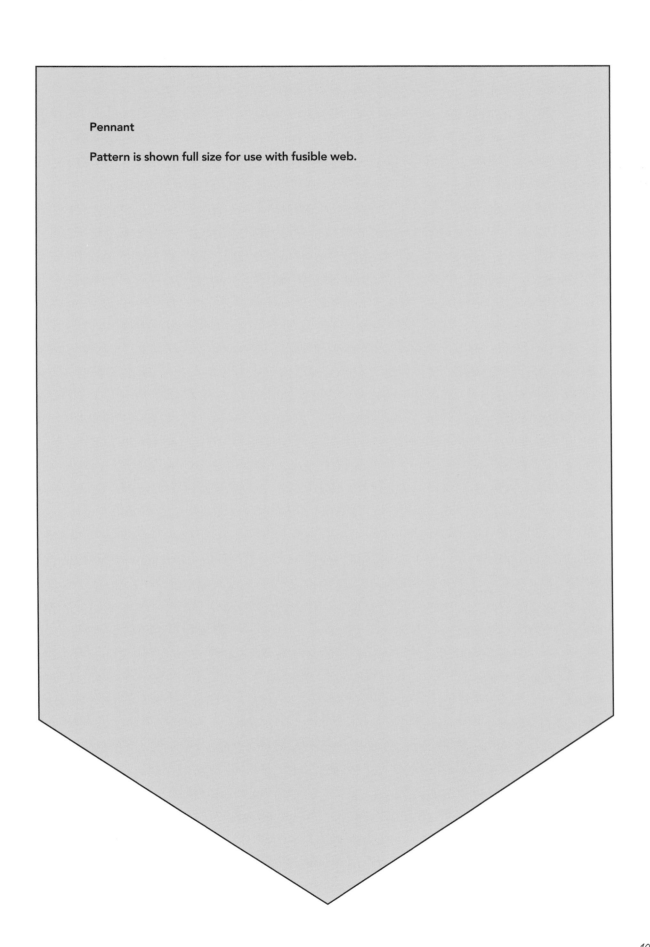

Pennant

Pattern is shown full size for use with fusible web.

Use this as either a table topper or wall hanging to display during the season of plenty.

THANKS *table topper*

Size: 24" diameter

MATERIALS

¾ yard rust print

12" square red print

12" square dark red print

½ yard brown print

1 fat quarter* light green print

6" square dark green print

1 fat quarter* orange print print

12" square gold print

Paper-backed fusible web

¾ yard backing fabric

28" square of quilt batting

Wire hanger (optional)

*fat quarter = 18" × 20"

Cutting

Measurements include ¼" seam allowances. Follow manufacturer's instructions for using fusible web.

FROM RUST PRINT, CUT:

- 1 Circle for background.
- 1 Half Circle.

FROM RED PRINT, CUT:

- 1 Medium Leaf.

FROM DARK RED PRINT, CUT:

- 1 Large Leaf.

FROM BROWN PRINT, CUT:

- 1 Thanks.
- 2 Pear Stems.
- 80" of 2¼"-wide bias strips. Join strips to make bias binding.

FROM LIGHT GREEN PRINT, CUT:

- 1 Gourd.
- 1 Small Leaf.

FROM DARK GREEN PRINT, CUT:

- 1 Pumpkin Stem.
- 1 Gourd Stem.

FROM ORANGE PRINT, CUT:

- 1 Pumpkin.

FROM GOLD PRINT, CUT:

- 1 Pears.

Quilt Assembly

1 Position appliqué pieces on rust print circle as shown in photo; fuse in place.

2 Machine appliqué using matching thread and satin stitch.

3 Stitch leaf veins and pumpkin and gourd details using satin stitch and matching thread.

Sew Smart™

Use tear-away stabilizer under your work to stabilize center-piece when doing machine satin stitching.—Patrick

Finishing

1 Layer backing, batting, and quilt top; baste. Quilt as desired.

2 Trim backing and batting even with edges of quilt top.

3 Hem straight edge of rust print half circle. Baste half circle to back of quilt, aligning curved top edges as shown in Back Diagram.

4 Add binding to quilt.

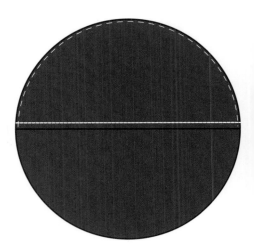

Back Diagram

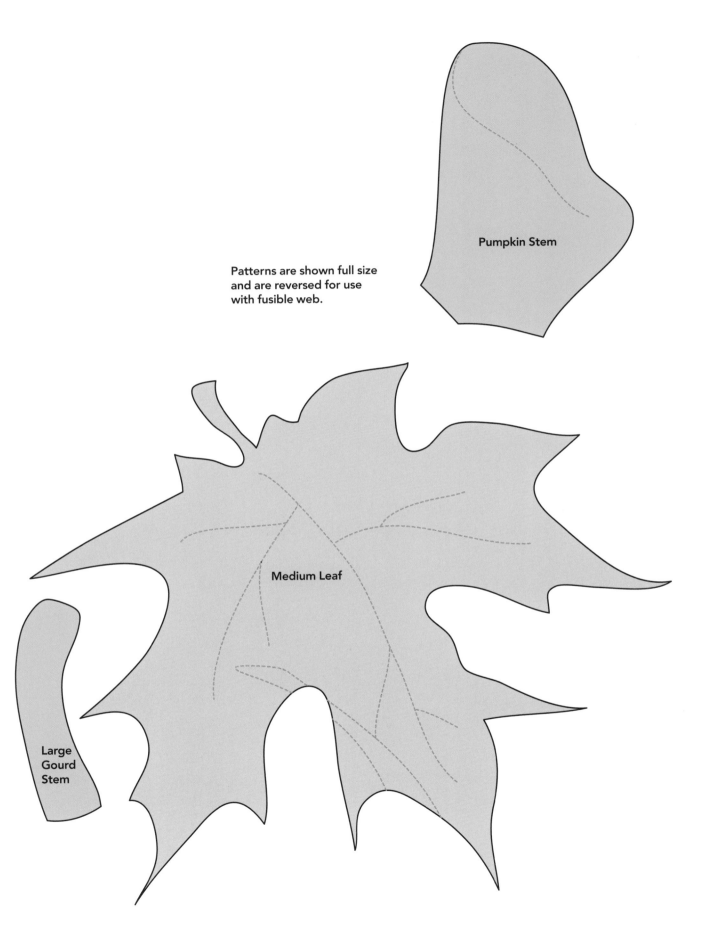

Pumpkin Stem

Patterns are shown full size
and are reversed for use
with fusible web.

Medium Leaf

Large
Gourd
Stem

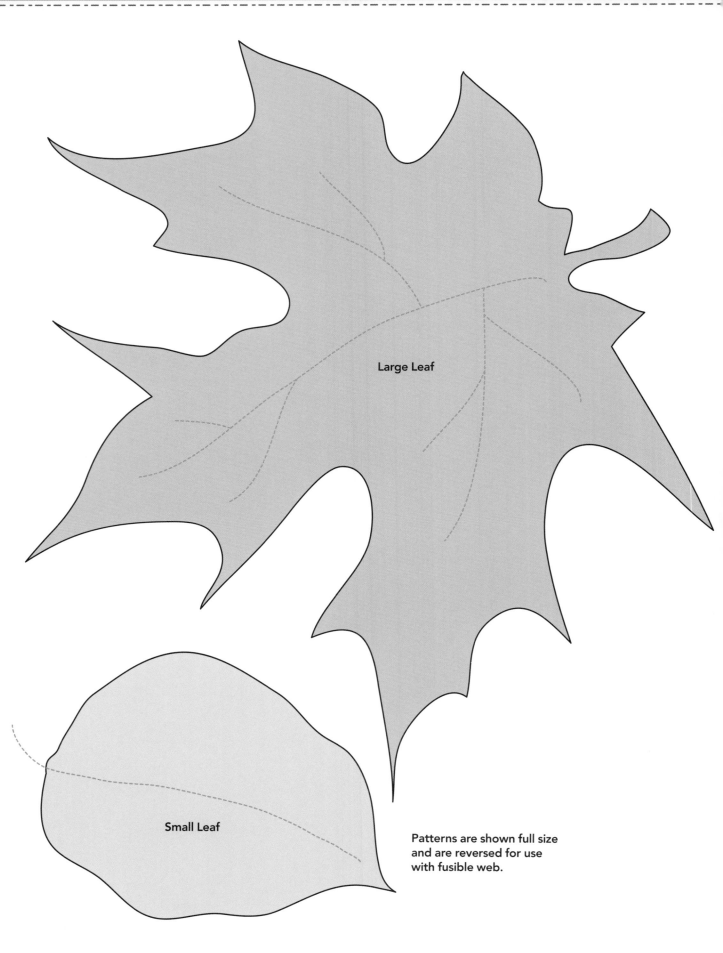

Large Leaf

Small Leaf

Patterns are shown full size
and are reversed for use
with fusible web.

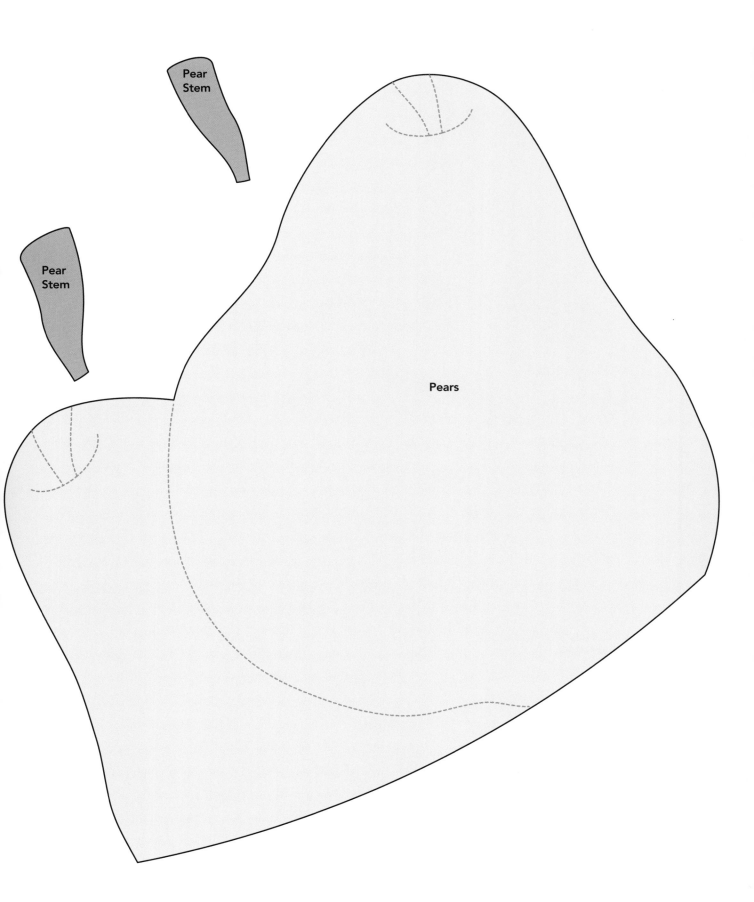

Pear
Stem

Pear
Stem

Pears

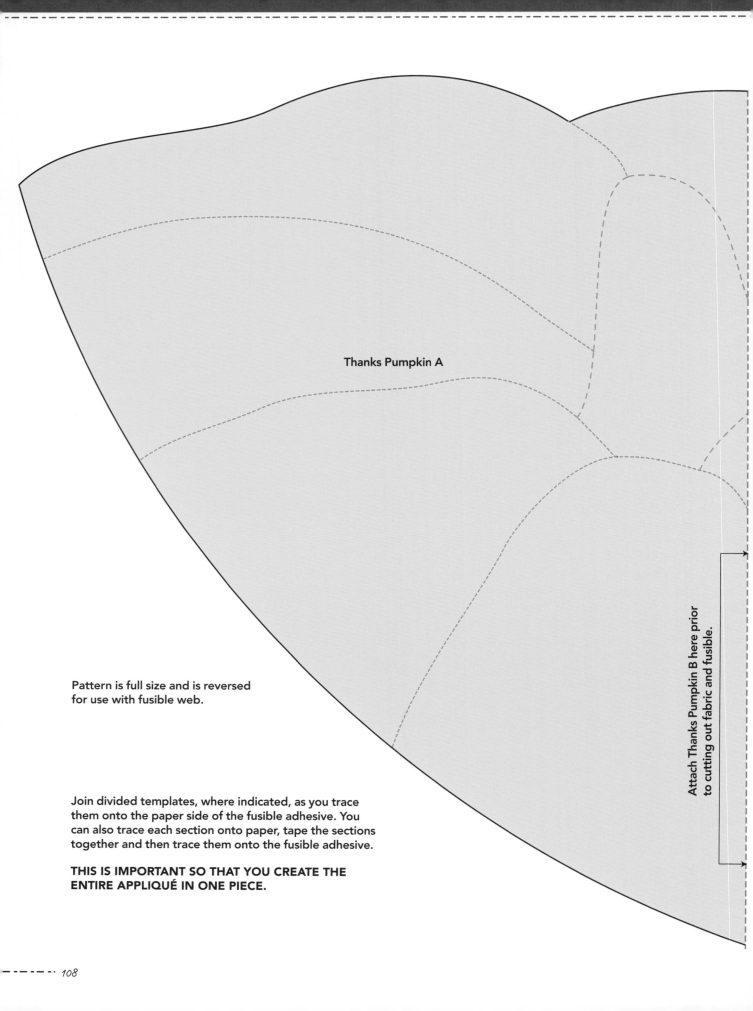

Thanks Pumpkin A

Pattern is full size and is reversed for use with fusible web.

Join divided templates, where indicated, as you trace them onto the paper side of the fusible adhesive. You can also trace each section onto paper, tape the sections together and then trace them onto the fusible adhesive.

THIS IS IMPORTANT SO THAT YOU CREATE THE ENTIRE APPLIQUÉ IN ONE PIECE.

Attach Thanks Pumpkin B here prior to cutting out fabric and fusible.

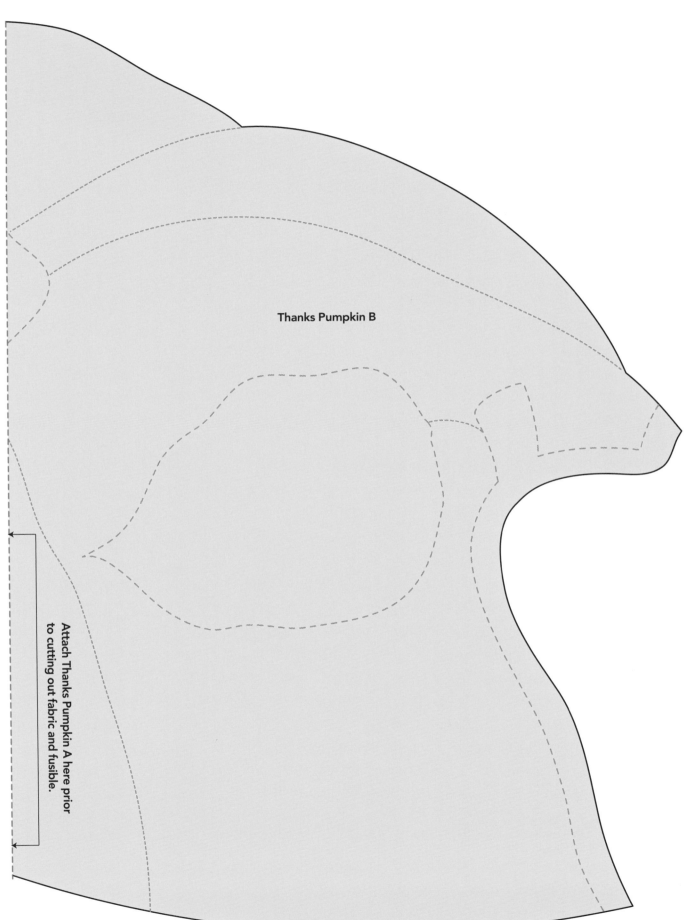

Thanks Pumpkin B

Attach Thanks Pumpkin A here prior to cutting out fabric and fusible.

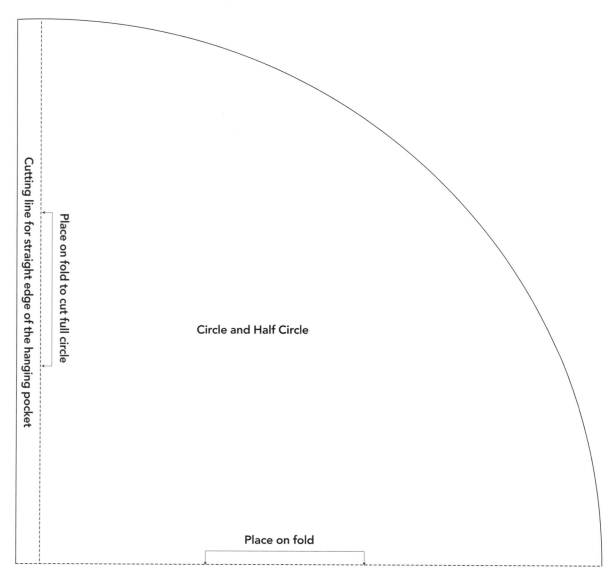

Cutting line for straight edge of the hanging pocket

Place on fold to cut full circle

Circle and Half Circle

Place on fold

Pattern is shown at 50%. Enlarge to 200% before using.

Pattern is shown at 50% and is
reversed for use with fusible web.
Enlarge to 200% and add ³⁄₁₆" seam
allowance for hand appliqué.

Fiery fall colors are the perfect palette for this warm and generously-sized throw quilt.

AUTUMN ABLAZE *throw*

Size: 72" × 72"
Blocks:
13 (12") Star blocks
12 (12") Leaf blocks

MATERIALS

1¾ yards gold print

1⅜ yards orange print

1⅛ yards dark red print

⅝ yard light brown print

3⅜ yards dark brown print

Paper-backed fusible web

4½ yards backing fabric

Full-size quilt batting

Web Extra

Machine embroidery appliqué design is available for this project. For ordering information, go to www.QuiltingCelebrations.com/embroidery.

Cutting

Measurements include ¼" seam allowances. Border strips are exact length needed. You may want to cut them longer to allow for piecing variations. Follow manufacturer's instructions for using fusible web.

FROM GOLD PRINT, CUT:

- 14 (3½"-wide) strips. From strips, cut 52 (3½" × 6½") C rectangles and 52 (3½") D squares.
- 4 Leaves.

FROM ORANGE PRINT, CUT:

- 10 (3½"-wide) strips. From strips, cut 104 (3½") D squares.
- 4 Leaves.

FROM DARK RED PRINT, CUT:

- 2 (4¾"-wide) strips. From strips, cut 13 (4¾") A squares.
- 7 (2½"-wide) strips. Piece strips to make 2 (2½" × 64½") top and bottom inner borders and 2 (2½" × 60½") side inner borders.
- 4 Leaves.

FROM LIGHT BROWN PRINT, CUT:

- 5 (3½"-wide) strips. From strips, cut 48 (3½") D squares.

FROM DARK BROWN PRINT, CUT:

- 4 (12½"-wide) strips. From strips, cut 12 (12½") background squares.
- 8 (4½"-wide) strips. Piece strips to make 2 (4½" × 72½") top and bottom outer borders and 2 (4½" × 64½") side outer borders.
- 3 (3⅞"-wide) strips. From strips, cut 26 (3⅞") squares. Cut squares in half diagonally to make 52 half-square B triangles.
- 8 (2¼"-wide) strips for binding.

Star Block Assembly

1 Join 1 dark red print A square and 4 dark brown print B triangles as shown in Center Unit Diagrams. Make 13 Center Units.

Center Unit Diagrams

Sew Smart™

Stitch units "assembly-line style" to save time. —Patrick

2 Referring to Star Point Unit Diagrams, place 1 orange print D square atop 1 gold print C rectangle, right sides facing. Stitch diagonally from corner to corner as shown. Trim ¼" beyond stitching. Press open to reveal triangle. Repeat for opposite end of rectangle to complete 1 Star Point Unit. Make 52 Star Point Units.

Star Point Unit Diagrams

3 Lay out 1 Center Unit, 4 Star Point Units, and 4 gold print D squares as shown in Star Block Assembly Diagram. Join into rows; join rows to complete 1 Star block (Star Block Diagram). Make 13 Star blocks.

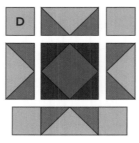

Star Block Assembly Diagram

Star Block Diagram

Leaf Block Assembly

1 Referring to Leaf Block Diagrams, place 1 light brown print D square atop 1 dark brown print background square, right sides facing. Stitch diagonally from corner to corner as shown. Trim ¼" beyond stitching. Press open to reveal triangle. Repeat for remaining corners to complete 1 background square. Make 12 background squares.

2 Position dark red print leaf atop 1 background square as shown in Leaf Block Diagrams. Fuse leaf in place. Machine appliqué leaves using matching thread and satin stitch. Make 4 dark red Leaf blocks.

3 Fuse orange and gold print leaves to dark brown print background squares as shown. Make 4 orange Leaf blocks and 4 gold Leaf blocks.

4 Machine appliqué leaves using matching thread and satin stitch.

5 Stitch leaf veins using satin stitch and matching thread.

Make 4
Leaf Block Diagrams

Quilt Assembly

1 Lay out blocks as shown in Quilt Top Assembly Diagram.

2 Join blocks into rows; join rows to complete quilt center.

3 Add dark red print side inner borders to quilt center. Add top and bottom inner borders to quilt.

4 Repeat for dark brown print outer borders.

Finishing

1 Divide backing into 2 (2¼-yard) lengths. Join panels lengthwise.

2 Layer backing, batting, and quilt top; baste. Quilt as desired.

3 Join 2¼"-wide dark brown print strips into 1 continuous piece for straight-grain French-fold binding. Add binding to quilt.

Quilt Top Assembly Diagram

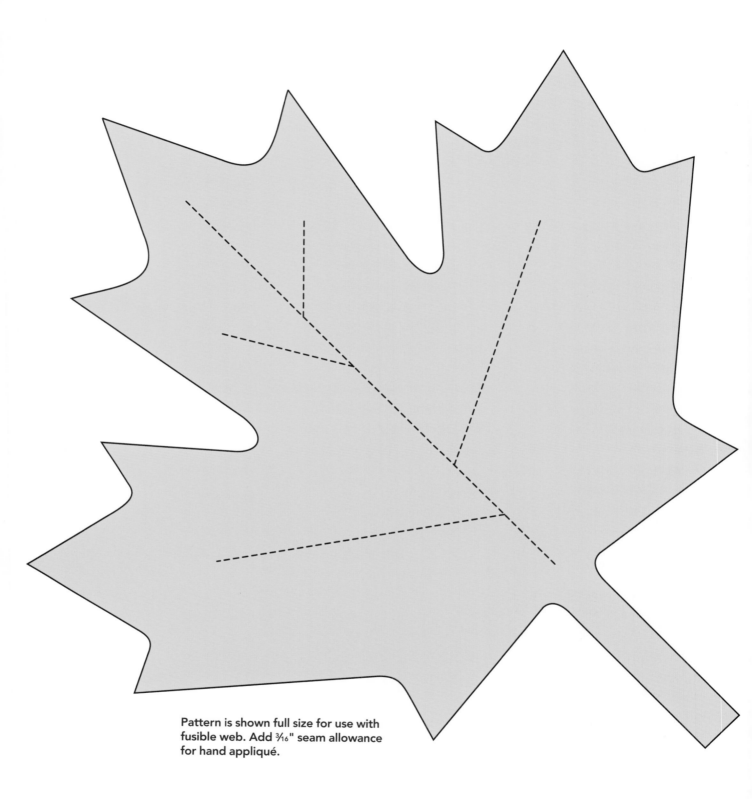

Pattern is shown full size for use with fusible web. Add ³⁄₁₆" seam allowance for hand appliqué.

Even a beginner can embroider these spirited stockings with simple running stitches and snowflakes.

STOCKINGS FOR STUFFING

MATERIALS

FOR STRIPED STOCKING

¾ yard red print

1 yard cream print

1 fat eighth* green print

Paper-backed fusible web

Pearl cotton in green and cream

2 (15" × 23") rectangles quilt batting

FOR MERRY STOCKING

¾ yard cream print

1 yard green print

1 fat eighth* red print

Paper-backed fusible web

Pearl cotton in red, green, and cream

2 (15" × 23") rectangles quilt batting

FOR CIRCLE STOCKING

¾ yard green print

1 yard red print

1 fat eighth* cream print

Paper-backed fusible web

Pearl cotton in red and cream

2 (15" × 23") rectangles quilt batting

*fat eighth = 9" × 20"

Cutting

Measurements include ¼" seam allowances. Follow manufacturer's instructions for using fusible web.

FOR STRIPED STOCKING
FROM RED PRINT, CUT:

- 1 Stocking (front).
- 1 Stocking reversed (back).

FROM CREAM PRINT, CUT:

- 2 (15" × 23") rectangles for lining.
- 80" of 2¼"-wide bias strips for binding and loop.
- 4 Stripes.

FROM GREEN PRINT, CUT:

- 4 Stripes.

FOR MERRY STOCKING
FROM CREAM PRINT, CUT:

- 1 Stocking (front).
- 1 Stocking reversed (back).

FROM GREEN PRINT, CUT:

- 2 (15" × 23") rectangles for lining.
- 80" of 2¼"-wide bias strips for binding and loop.
- 1 each E and R.

FROM RED PRINT, CUT:

- 1 each M, R, and Y.

FOR CIRCLE STOCKING
FROM GREEN PRINT, CUT:

- 1 Stocking (front).
- 1 Stocking reversed (back).

FROM RED PRINT, CUT:

- 2 (15" × 23") rectangles for lining.
- 80" of 2¼"-wide bias strips for binding and loop.
- 2 Large Circles.
- 1 Small Circle.

FROM CREAM PRINT, CUT:

- 2 Large Circles.
- 2 Small Circles.

Assembly

FOR ALL STOCKINGS:

1 Referring to photos, arrange appliqué pieces atop stocking front.

2 Fuse pieces in place.

Finishing

1 Layer lining rectangle, batting, and stocking front; baste.

2 Quilt as desired. Stockings shown were quilted with stippling and meandering. Trim lining and batting even with edges of stocking front.

3 Stitching through all layers, machine appliqué using satin stitch and matching thread.

4 In the same manner, layer lining rectangle, batting, and stocking back; baste. Quilt as desired. Trim lining and batting even with edges of stocking back.

5 **For Merry Stocking:** using red and green pearl cotton, outline letters using running stitch (Running Stitch Diagram). Stitch snowflakes on letters using cream pearl cotton (Snowflake Diagram).

For Striped Stocking: using cream pearl cotton and running stitch, stitch above and below pairs of green stripes. Repeat using green pearl cotton above and below pairs of cream stripes. Stitch snowflakes between stripes.

For Circle Stocking: using cream pearl cotton and running stitch, outline red circles. Repeat using red pearl cotton to outline cream circles. Stitch snowflakes on circles.

6 Place stocking front atop stocking back, wrong sides facing. Baste together around sides and bottom.

7 Add binding to sides and bottom of stocking.

8 Add binding to top of stocking, leaving a 5" tail. Whipstitch seam of tail closed. Fold tail toward inside of stocking; tack in place to make hanging loop.

Running Stitch Diagram

Snowflake Diagram

Patterns are shown full size and are reversed for use with fusible web. Add ³⁄₁₆" seam allowance for hand appliqué.

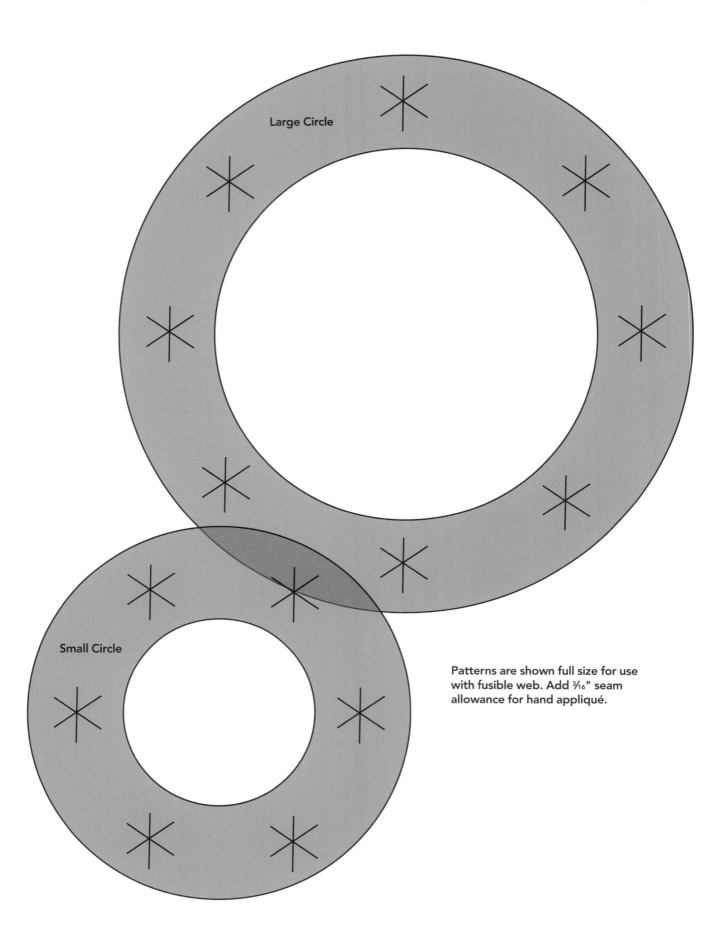

Large Circle

Small Circle

Patterns are shown full size for use
with fusible web. Add ³⁄₁₆" seam
allowance for hand appliqué.

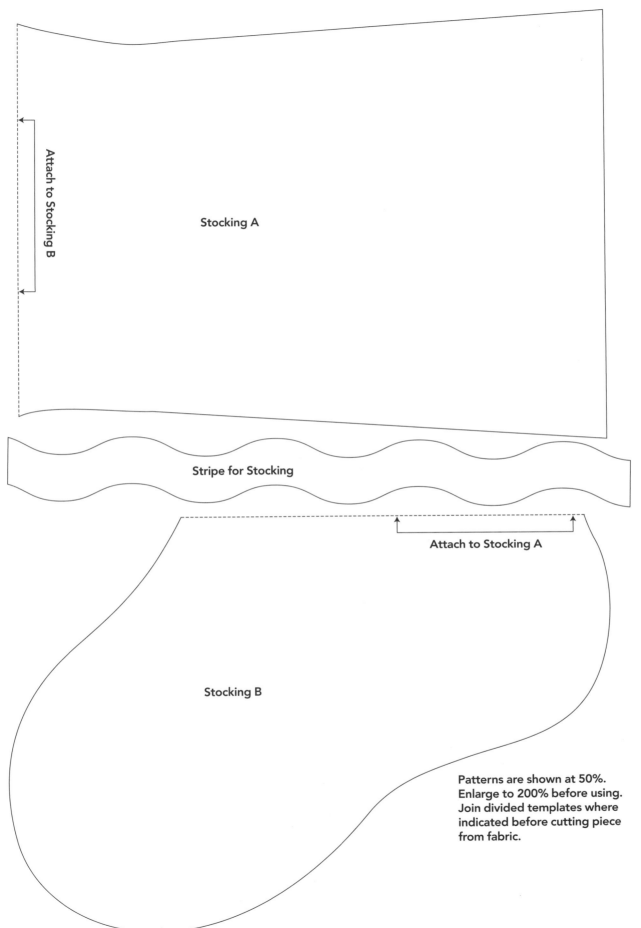

Attach to Stocking B

Stocking A

Stripe for Stocking

Attach to Stocking A

Stocking B

Patterns are shown at 50%. Enlarge to 200% before using. Join divided templates where indicated before cutting piece from fabric.

Hand appliqué, and traditional piecing help to evoke a sense of Christmas past in this striking quilt with a vintage air.

CANDY-STRIPED CHRISTMAS *quilt*

Size: 102" × 102"
Blocks:
16 (13½") Courthouse Steps blocks
9 (13½") Star blocks

MATERIALS

1¾ yards light green print

1¼ yards dark green print

1¾ yards light red print

¾ yard dark red print

2¾ yards ivory print

5 yards cream print

Paper-backed fusible web (optional)

9 yards backing fabric

King-size quilt batting

Cutting

Measurements include ¼" seam allowances. Follow manufacturer's instructions if using fusible web.

FROM LIGHT GREEN PRINT, CUT:

- 16 (2"-wide) strips. From strips, cut 24 (2" × 14") E rectangles, 24 (2" × 11") D rectangles, and 8 (2") A squares.

- 11 (2¼"-wide) strips for binding.

FROM DARK GREEN PRINT, CUT:

- 17 (2"-wide) strips. From 6 strips, cut 16 (2" × 8") C rectangles and 16 (2" × 5") B rectangles. Piece remaining strips to make 4 (2" × 106") border strips.

- 4 Stars.

FROM LIGHT RED PRINT, CUT:

- 29 (2"-wide) strips. From 18 strips, cut 26 (2" × 14") E rectangles and 26 (2" × 11") D rectangles, and 8 (2") A squares. Piece remaining strips to make 4 (2" × 106") border strips.

FROM DARK RED PRINT, CUT:

- 6 (2"-wide) strips. From strips, cut 16 (2" × 8") C rectangles and 16 (2" × 5") B rectangles.

- 5 Stars.

FROM IVORY PRINT, CUT:

- 3 (11"-wide) strips. From strips, cut 9 (11") background squares.

- 29 (2"-wide) strips. From 18 strips, cut 32 (2" × 11") D rectangles and 32 (2" × 8") C rectangles. Piece remaining strips to make 4 (2" × 106") border strips.

FROM CREAM PRINT, CUT:

- 2 (14"-wide) strips. From strips, cut 20 (14" × 3½") horizontal sashing strips.

- 17 (2"-wide) strips. From 6 strips, cut 32 (2" × 5") B rectangles and 32 (2") A squares. Piece remaining strips to make 4 (2" × 106") border strips.

FROM REMAINDER OF CREAM PRINT, CUT:

- 4 (5¾"-wide) lengthwise strips. From strips, cut 4 (5¾" × 106") border strips.

- 4 (3½"-wide) lengthwise strips. From strips, cut 4 (3½" × 80") vertical sashing strips.

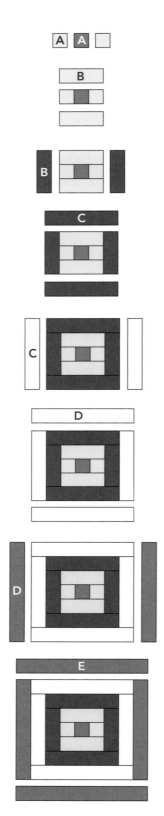

Block Assembly

1 Lay out 1 set of light green, cream, dark green, and ivory print pieces as shown in Courthouse Steps Block Assembly Diagrams. Join pieces in alphabetical order to complete 1 green Courthouse Steps block (Courthouse Steps Block Diagrams). Make 8 green Courthouse Steps blocks.

Sew Smart™

Stitch blocks "assembly-line style" to save time.—Patrick

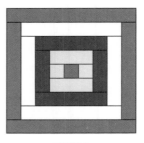

MAKE 8

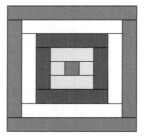

MAKE 8

Courthouse Steps Block Assembly Diagrams

Courthouse Steps Block Diagrams

2 In the same manner, make 8 red Courthouse Steps blocks.

3 Center 1 dark red print star atop 1 ivory print background square as shown in Star Block Assembly Diagrams. Appliqué in place.

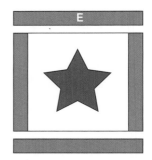

Star Block Assembly Diagrams

Sew Smart™

See Needle-Turn Appliqué in the Techniques section at the end of the book.—Patrick

5 Add 2 light red print D rectangles and 2 light red print E rectangles to sides of square to complete 1 Star block as shown in Star Block Diagrams. Make 5 red Star blocks.

6 In the same manner, make 4 green Star blocks using 1 ivory background square, 1 dark green print star, 2 light green print D rectangles, and 2 light green print E rectangles in each.

MAKE 5

MAKE 4

Star Block Diagrams

Quilt Assembly

1 Lay out blocks and sashing strips as shown in Quilt Top Assembly Diagram.

2 Join blocks and horizontal sashing strips into vertical rows; join rows and vertical sashing strips to complete quilt center.

3 Referring to Quilt Top Assembly Diagram, join 1 (5¾"-wide) cream print border strip, 1 dark green print border strip, 1 ivory print border strip, 1 light red print border strip, and 1 (2"-wide) cream print border strip to make 1 border. Make 4 borders.

4 Add borders to quilt, mitering corners.

Sew Smart™

See Mitered Borders in the Techniques section at the end of the book.—Patrick

Quilt Top Assembly Diagram

Finishing

1 Divide backing into 3 (3-yard) lengths. Join panels lengthwise.

2 Layer backing, batting, and quilt top; baste. Quilt as desired.

3 Join 2¼"-wide light green print strips into 1 continuous piece for straight-grain French-fold binding. Add binding to quilt.

Pattern is shown full size for use with fusible web. Add ³⁄₁₆" seam allowance for hand appliqué.

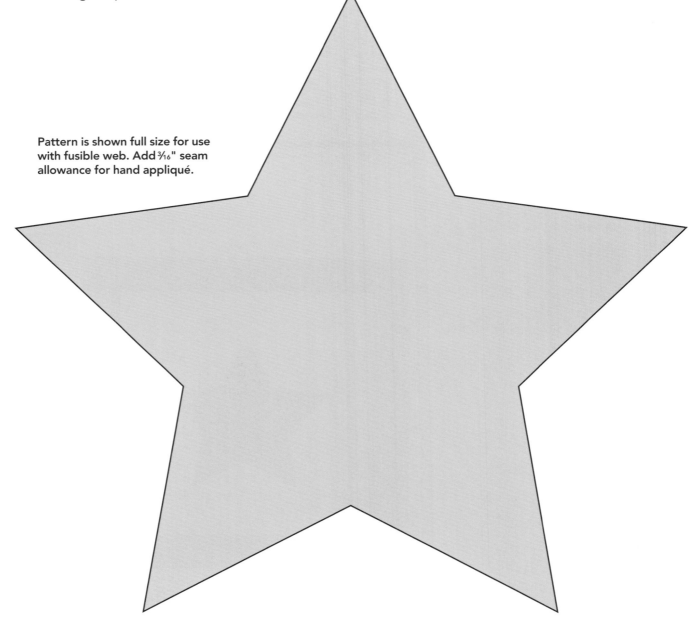

THE BASICS

Read the instructions thoroughly before you begin cutting and sewing. All the projects in this book are pieced using a ¼" seam with the fabrics placed right sides together unless otherwise noted.

Tools

Gather all the necessary tools before you start cutting and stitching. Below is a list of tools that will make your work easier.

- Rotary cutter and cutting mat.
- Transparent acrylic gridded ruler.
- Sewing machine capable of doing a narrow zigzag or satin stitch.
- Paper scissors.
- Fabric scissors.
- Sewing machine needles—size 90/14 universal titanium needles are great, but not necessary.
- A variety of threads for appliqué and quilting.
- Iron and ironing board.
- Darning foot for free-motion quilting.
- Safety pins.
- Lite Steam-A-Seam 2 paper-backed fusible web.
- Appliqué pressing sheet.
- Tear-away stabilizer.

Fabrics

If you prewash your fabric, use warm water to allow the fabric to shrink as much as it is going to. Tumble dry the fabric, and remove it from the dryer when it is still slightly damp. Always iron your fabric before measuring and cutting. Do not use starch on fabrics that will be used in appliqué pieces. It may make the fabric difficult to fuse.

It is extremely important to measure and cut your fabrics accurately and to stitch using an exact ¼" seam. You're sure to be proud of your finished piece if you follow these simple rules.

Appliqué

Most of the appliqué projects in this magazine use a fused method and satin stitching to finish the raw edges. If you wish to do hand appliqué you'll need to trace the printed templates in mirror image and add seam allowances to them. Place appliqué templates on the right side of the fabric for cutting.

Fusible Appliqué Preparations

Templates are printed actual size unless otherwise indicated and are reversed for tracing onto fusible web. Be sure to use a lightweight, paper-backed fusible web that is suitable for sewing.

If necessary, join the pieces as indicated on the template before tracing on fusible web.

Sew Smart™

I choose Lite Steam-A-Seam 2 because I know it stays fused well in raw edge appliqué. —Patrick

1 Place the fusible web, paper side up, over each template piece, and trace the shape onto the paper side. Write the name, piece number, and fabric color on each piece as you trace it.

NOTE: In places where the pieces butt up to one another, overlapping them will keep them from gapping.

Either cut the pieces the exact size and then overlap slightly, or add approximately 1/16" to the underneath piece. The latter method will add some bulk to your project, but works well if you are new to satin stitching.

2 Roughly cut all the pieces approximately 1/4" outside the traced lines.

3 Following the manufacturer's instructions for the fusible web, fuse the traced pattern pieces onto the wrong side of fabric.

4 Cut out pieces neatly along the traced lines.

5 Transfer any placement and stitching lines to the right side of the fabric using a lightbox and a pencil.

6 Arrange all of the appliqué pieces as pictured. When you're satisfied with the arrangement, fuse them to the background.

TiP

If the project includes light-colored pieces that will be placed on top of a dark layer or background, fuse two layers of the light fabric together to prevent the dark color from showing through. Then, fuse the traced pattern to the back of the bottom light layer. To determine if this will be necessary, simply check the transparency of your lighter fabric by laying it over the darker fabric.

TiP

Be sure to layer and arrange all the pieces on the background before fusing any of them.

Layering and Quilting

Cut your backing fabric and batting to measure an inch or two larger than your quilt top on all sides. Sandwich the batting between the quilt top and the backing, wrong sides together, and baste through all the layers, smoothing the quilt top outward from the center. You can also use safety pins spaced 4" to 6" apart.

All the quilting in this book was done by machine. Use a walking foot for straight-line quilting. For free-motion or stipple quilting, use a darning foot and lower the feed dogs on your machine. Quilt as desired, or refer to the photos that are included with each project.

Sew Smart™

I like to use a single layer of thin cotton batting such as Warm & Natural.—Patrick

Sew Smart™

A Clover Chaco Liner is great for marking quilting lines if you are not comfortable stitching them freehand. The chalk lines can be easily brushed away.—Patrick

BINDING

I have a little binding trick that I teach my students, and they always tell me that learning it is worth the fee they paid for the class. It involves cutting out a little of the bulk at the corners (similar to the way that clipping and grading works on a garment seam in fashion sewing).

I've seen many students who, after stitching their binding on, whack the corner off of the quilt with a diagonal cut beyond the seam line. What they removed with that cut was actually the foundation for a good corner. Don't do that! Instead, use my binding instructions to remove just a little bit that makes a big difference. These tips and techniques will help you get perfect corners on your binding.

1 Begin stitching the binding to the quilt approximately 6"–8" from the beginning of the binding strip, using a ¼" seam allowance.

2 Stitch to ¼" from the corner; stop with needle in down position.

3 Raise presser foot, pivot quilt, and stitch a line from this point through the corner of the quilt as shown. Do not backstitch.

4 Fold the binding up, along the diagonal stitching line.

5 Fold binding down to align with the next edge to be stitched. Continue stitching around the quilt, repeating steps #2–#5 for each corner.

6 Stop stitching about 8"–10" from where you started. Fold binding back, butting the fold up to the beginning of the binding strip.

7 To the left of the fold, mark the binding at whatever the measurement is for the width of your binding. (For 2¼"-wide binding mark a line 2¼" to the left of the fold.)

8 Cut away the excess binding beyond the marked line.

9 Open up the binding and place the two ends right sides together at a right angle as shown. The wrong side of the beginning end of the binding should face up.

10 Pin the binding strips together and mark a stitching line from corner to corner. Stitch along marked line to join the binding ends with a mitered seam. Trim ¼" beyond stitching. Press seam. Refold binding on crease. Finish stitching binding to quilt.

11 At each corner, slip the point of your scissors under the fold in the binding. Snip to the stitching line, but not beyond it. Lift up the seam allowance of the binding layers to reveal the diagonal seam stitched in Step #3. Remove the stitching of the diagonal seam.

12 You have created a wedge of fabric that will be removed.

13 Pull the binding and the quilt seam allowances away from this wedge from above and below it.

14 Cut away the wedge to the right of the seam line, being careful not to cut the binding or quilt.

15 Press binding away from quilt top and turn to the back, forming an angled fold.

16 Pin or clip turned binding in place. Turn quilt to back side and turn the next side of the binding over as shown to make a neatly mitered corner. Pin or clip binding in place and stitch to quilt back by hand.

HAND-STITCHED BINDING

One of the biggest milestones on the road to my becoming a better quilter was convincing myself that, after years of stitching the bindings to the backs of my quilts by machine, it just isn't always the best method. No matter how much I tried to rationalize my way out of it by telling myself things like, "You're not making competition quilts here," or "this one's no heirloom," I finally realized that I would never be as proud of the end result as I would be if I just bit the bullet and did it by hand.

If you've always used your machine for binding, and you'd like to give handstitching a try, use this method to give your bindings that perfect finishing touch. With a little patience and practice, you'll soon be stitching your binding by hand.

Start with a very sharp needle and a manageable length of thread. I usually use a #9 or #10 appliqué needle, but straw needles also work well. An old rule of thumb is to never use a thread longer than the distance from your wrist to your elbow. I usually work with about 18" because longer threads tangle more easily. Thread your needle, knot the thread, and proceed as follows:

1 Fold the binding over the raw edge of the quilt to the back and hold it in place with your left hand. Your first stitch should be made within the seam allowance to hide the knot. Take a stitch outside of the seamline. The length of your stitch should be about ¼".

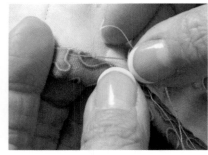

2 Catching just a couple of threads, bring the needle up through the fold of the binding directly across from where you exited the backing, or just to the underside of the fold to make it even less visible.

3 Pull the thread through the binding until it's snug.

4 Begin your next stitch into the backing where you exited it before and take another ¼" stitch as in Step 1.

5 As you become more proficient, your needle will exit the backing and enter the binding fold almost simultaneously. It is important to make the stitch in and out of the binding directly in line with the entry/exit points in the quilt's backing. This will keep the stitches nearly invisible. Continue in this manner around the entire quilt. Miter corners by folding them in the opposite direction of the folds on the front side of the quilt.

MAKING CONTINUOUS BIAS BINDING

Determine the size of fabric square you'll need

1 Measure the circumference of your quilt. Add the length of binding you need for connecting or overlapping the ends (about 20"). If you are binding multiple smaller pieces, add their circumferences together.

Sew Smart™

When you're making several curved-edge placemats, table toppers or mug mats, you can cut enough binding for all of them from a single square of fabric.—Patrick

2 Multiply the total length of the binding strip needed by your desired binding width. This will give you the binding area in square inches.

3 Calculate the square root of the area. (Use a calculator with a square root function.)

FOR EXAMPLE:
If you need a bias strip that is 112" long and 2¼" (2.25") wide:

Multiply 112 × 2.25. That equals 252 square inches.

The square root of 252 is 15.87. Round up to 16.

Cut a 16" square of fabric for your bias binding.

Sew Smart™

Be careful not to stretch bias binding as you apply it to your project.—Patrick

Create a continuous bias binding strip

1 Cut the fabric square in half diagonally. Place the two triangle pieces right sides together with the straight edges on the right as shown in Diagram A. Press seam open.

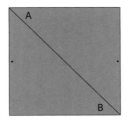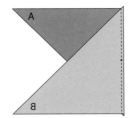

Diagram A

2 Using a gridded transparent ruler, measure from the long diagonal edge and draw a parallel line every 2¼" on the wrong side of the fabric piece as shown in Diagram B.

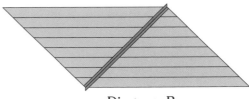

Diagram B

3 Fold the marked piece right sides together to form a tube, aligning the edges and pinning the marked lines so one width of the binding extends beyond the edge on each side as shown in Diagram C. Sew the tube together with a ¼" seam; press the seam open. Cut on the marked line to make one continuous 2¼"-wide bias binding strip.

Diagram C

MITERED BORDERS

The subtle seam of a mitered corner creates the illusion of a continuous line around the quilt. Mitered corners are ideal for striped fabric borders or multiple plain borders.

1 Referring to Measuring Quilt Center Diagram, measure your quilt length through the middle of the quilt rather than along the edges. In the same manner, measure quilt width. Add to your measurements twice the planned width of the border plus 2". Trim borders to these measurements.

Measuring Quilt Center Diagram

2 On wrong side of quilt top, mark ¼" seam allowances at each corner.

3 Fold quilt top in half and place a pin at the center of the quilt side. Fold border in half and mark center with pin.

4 With right sides facing and raw edges aligned, match center pins on the border and the quilt. Working from the center out, pin the border to the quilt, right sides facing. The border will extend beyond the quilt edges. Do not trim the border.

5 Sew the border to the quilt. Start and stop stitching ¼" from the corner of the quilt top, backstitching at each end. Press the seam allowance toward the border. Add the remaining borders in the same manner.

6 With right sides facing, fold the quilt diagonally as shown in Mitering Diagram 1, aligning the raw edges of the adjacent borders. Pin securely.

Mitering Diagram 1

7 Align a ruler along the diagonal fold, as shown in Mitering Diagram 2. Holding the ruler firmly, mark a line from the end of the border seam to the raw edge.

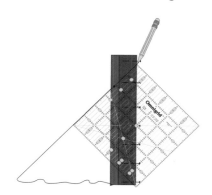

Mitering Diagram 2

8 Start machine-stitching at the beginning of the marked line, backstitch, and then stitch on the line out to the raw edge.

9 Unfold the quilt to be sure that the corner lies flat (Mitered Borders Diagram). Correct the stitching if necessary. Trim the seam allowance to ¼".

Mitered Borders Diagram

10 Miter the remaining corners. Press the corner seams open.

WINDOWING FUSIBLE APPLIQUÉ

To reduce bulk and stiffness in your appliqué, try windowing the fusible web. Use only a thin ring of adhesive, and fuse just the outermost edges of your appliqué shapes, keeping them soft to the touch. Follow the steps in this photo tutorial to create fusible appliqué quilts that drape nicely.

1 Trace appliqué template(s) on the paper side of fusible adhesive. Leave approximately 1" of space between shapes. I use a fine point permanent marker for tracing to avoid getting pencil lead on my hands or fabrics.

2 Cut out the traced shapes from the fusible adhesive, about ½" outside the traced line.

3 Cut about ¼" inside the traced line to remove the center of the fusible adhesive.

4 Place the fusible adhesive on the wrong side of your appliqué fabric and, when you are satisfied with the positioning, fuse into place according to the manufacturer's instructions. Do not remove the paper backing.

5 Cut out appliqués on the traced lines. Remove the paper backing when ready for placement.

NEEDLE-TURN APPLIQUÉ

Needle-turn appliqué derives its name from the action of turning under the seam allowance edge of appliqué pieces with the needle used for stitching. Use a blindstitch to secure the folded edge of fabric to a background.

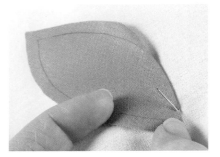

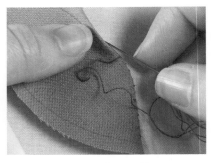

1 Pull needle and knotted thread up through background fabric and folded edge of appliqué piece, barely catching edge of fold.

Sew Smart™

Use thread to match your appliqué piece. Photos show stitching with contrasting thread for visibility. —Patrick

2 Reinsert needle into background fabric beside folded edge where thread was first brought through, and make a ⅛" stitch, bringing point of needle back up through background fabric and through folded edge of appliqué piece.

NOTE: As you begin each stitch, make sure needle enters background fabric right next to thread coming up through folded edge of appliqué.

3 Use point of needle to turn under a small portion of the appliqué piece seam allowance, using needle to smooth curves in folded edge

Sew Smart™

Pull each stitch to keep it tight, but do not pucker background fabric. —Patrick

4 Stitch to outer points; take a small extra stitch directly at the point. Use needle to turn seam allowance under on other side of point and continue stitching.

Stitches on top should be nearly invisible. Stitches on back side of background fabric should be straight and approximately ⅛" long (see photo above, right).

INVISIBLE MACHINE APPLIQUÉ

Use Kim Diehl's techniques for preparing appliqué shapes and setting up your sewing machine for invisible machine appliqué.

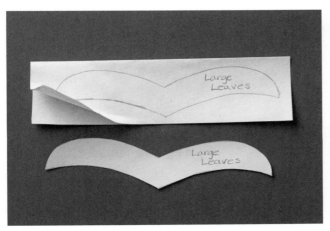

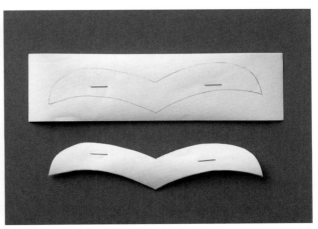

1 For each shape, cut a piece of freezer paper about twice as big as shape; trace shape onto one end of paper on the dull side. Fold paper with shiny sides facing and fuse together with a hot, dry iron. Cut out shape on the drawn line to make a template.

2 Trace around each template the required number of times on the dull side of freezer paper; cut on drawn line for pattern pieces. To make multiples, stack up to seven pieces of freezer paper underneath top traced sheet, anchor the layers with straight pins or staples, and cut on drawn line.

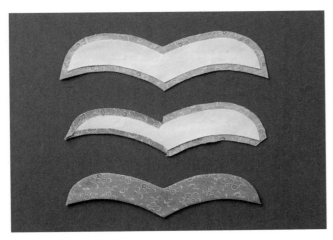

4 Prepare machine for invisible appliqué with mono-filament in needle and neutral all-purpose thread in bobbin. Set machine to sew a small zigzag stitch and adjust tension as needed so bobbin thread does not pull to the front of appliqués. For most machines, this will be a stitch width and length of 1 and a top tension of 1 to 2.

3 To cut appliqué shapes, use a sparing amount of fabric glue stick on the dull side of each pattern piece to anchor it to the wrong side of fabric, shiny side up. Cut out shapes, adding a scant ¼" seam allowance. Use a hot, dry iron to iron the seam allowance over onto the shiny side of each pattern piece, clipping inner curves and points nearly to the paper.

ADDING A HANGING SLEEVE

Use these instructions to make a hanging sleeve for the quilts in this book. The sleeve will accomodate a ½"-diameter dowel.

1 Cut a fabric strip 3½" wide × the quilt width measurement.

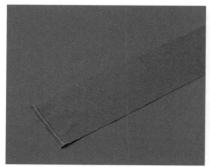

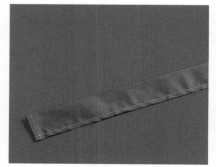

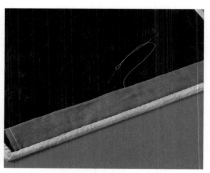

2 On each short side, fold under ¼" to the wrong side; press. Fold under another ¼" and press. Stitch close to the folded edges to make a rolled hem on each end.

3 Fold the sleeve in half lengthwise, wrong sides together, and stitch using a ¼" seam allowance. Press with seam centered on back side of sleeve.

4 Whipstitch the long sides of the sleeve to the back of the quilt, just under the binding.

SATIN STITCHING

Satin stitching by machine is one way to stitch around appliqués to secure them. The basic pointers here will help make this technique easier for you. Spend some time practicing and fine-tuning your satin stitching, and you'll be very happy with the new things you can do to embellish and adorn your projects.

In this lesson, we'll focus on the method used to create the smaller pieces, such as the fusible appliqué banners and table toppers.

Since the backs of these pieces will always be against a table or wall, don't worry about whether or not the satin stitching shows on them. Along with the quilting, you may chosse to do the satin stitching through the sandwiched layers of the quilt.

Satin stitching through all of the layers eliminates the need

for any tear-away stabilizer that would be necessary to satin stitch through a single layer of background fabric. This eliminates an extra step in the process. If you satin stitch your appliqués using stabilizer before putting your quilt top together, you'll still need to quilt them once you sandwich your layers.

The sandwiched piece can also be easier to maneuver because it has some body to it. As you do when you're quilting, roll up whatever part of a

piece you're not quilting or satin stitching and use the roll as the means for turning and manipulating the piece through the machine—much like the rudder on a boat.

But none of this matters at all if you're not yet comfortable with your satin stitching. So, keep these things in mind and use the tips that follow as a guide to learn and practice what makes this particular kind of appliqué look as if it's been embroidered.

Tips for Satin Stitching

1 Threads that are good for embroidery are good for satin stitching. Polyester threads or 40 wt rayon work well. The polyester is less prone to breakage than the rayon.

2 Your needle is also important. A 90/14 needle is great for satin stitching through the sandwiched layers, but wouldn't be good when used with a single layer of foundation fabric and stabilizer.

3 Set your machine to its zigzag or satin stitch setting, and adjust your stitch width as desired. Make sure the stitch is wide enough to stitch to the inside and outside of the raw edge of your appliqué. Use the 2.5 mm setting most often. On finer pieces and fabrics, use a narrower stitch. The narrower your stitch, the easier it is to make clean, tight curves. Satin stitching that is too wide is just not attractive.

4 The tighter your stitch length, the better. A tight stitch means it takes longer to go around your appliqué, but it's worth the time. Many students are unhappy with their satin stitching because they're too impatient to use the tightest stitch length possible. Set your stitch length at 0.2 mm for satin stitching. Your machine may not allow you to go that tight, so shorten your stitch length as much as possible. Experiment by lengthening the stitch slightly until it feeds smoothly.

5 Use an open-toe presser foot with a channel on the underside that allows your raised satin stitching to slide under it as you feed the piece through the machine. Guide the raw edge of your appliqué into the center mark on the foot to be sure you're encasing the entire raw edge of the fabric with your satin stitching.

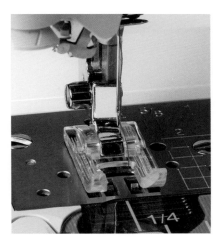

6 Stitch at a comfortable pace. Start slowly if you're a novice. As your stitching improves with practice, stitch faster. The faster you are able to stitch, the better your satin stitching will look. Many of today's home embroidery machines do the best satin stitching because they're made for that. With practice, you can make a basic machine with a zigzag stitch work well, too.

7 Satin stitching may come undone if the beginnings and endings aren't backstitched. Pull your thread tail to the front of the presser foot at the beginning of a line of satin stitching and stitch over it for an inch or so to keep it from coming undone and to hide the end.

8 Set your machine to stop with the needle in the down position when satin stitching to make pivoting easier.

9 Stitch over the raw edge with the appliqué to the left side of the needle.

Index

About the Author

Patrick has spent his professional years in a variety of creative fields. A prolific designer, he is probably most well known for his very successful and long-running collections of fabric from Timeless Treasures, Robert Kaufman Fabrics, and Moda that include his trademark marbleized solids which are trendsetters in the industry.

Patrick's quilts, crafts, clothing, and home decorating accessories have appeared in such distinguished magazines as *Better Homes & Gardens*, *American Patchwork and Quilting*, *Country Crafts* and many more. He has also written books on quilting and crafting and has appeared on several television programs. Look for Patrick's magazine, *Quilting Celebrations*, in quilt shops and on newsstands everywhere. His companion show to the magazine, "Quilting Celebrations with Patrick Lose" can be seen on QNNtv.com.

www.fwmedia.com

18 17 16 15 14   5 4 3 2 1

DISTRIBUTED IN CANADA BY FRASER DIRECT
100 Armstrong Avenue
Georgetown, ON, Canada L7G 5S4
Tel: (905) 877-4411

DISTRIBUTED IN THE U.K. AND EUROPE BY F&W MEDIA INTERNATIONAL
Brunel House, Newton Abbot, Devon, TQ12 4PU, England
Tel: (+44) 1626 323200, Fax: (+44) 1626 323319
Email: enquiries@fwmedia.com

DISTRIBUTED IN AUSTRALIA BY CAPRICORN LINK
P.O. Box 704, S. Windsor NSW, 2756 Australia
Tel: (02) 4560 1600, Fax: (02) 4577 5288
E-mail: books@capricornlink.com.au

SRN: T5658
ISBN-13: 978-1-4402-4351-6

Edited by the editors of *Quilting Celebrations*, *Love of Quilting* and Stephanie White
Designed by Brianna Scharstein
Production coordinated by Greg Nock
Photography by Dean Tanner

The fabric backgrounds featured in this book are from "Basically Patrick" collection by RJR Fabrics. Visit www.patricklose.com for more information.

METRIC CONVERSION CHART

CONVERT	TO	MULTIPLY BY
Inches	Centimeters	2.54
Centimeters	Inches	0.4
Feet	Centimeters	30.5
Centimeters	Feet	0.03
Yards	Meters	0.9
Meters	Yards	1.1

Keep Quilting with Fons & Porter!

Love of Quilting

Love of Quilting magazine is known for clear and accurate instructions, inspiring projects, and helpful hints, tips, and techniques. Marianne Fons and Liz Porter are two of the most trusted educators in quilting, and they bring their knowledge and skills to every issue of *Fons & Porter's Love of Quilting*.

Quilting Celebrations with Patrick Lose

If you love creating useful and decorative quilted pieces for all of life's good times as much as celebrating them, then *Quilting Celebrations* is just what you've been waiting for! Quilts, seasonal door banners and table toppers for the holidays are the types of projects you'll find in this magazine.

Do you need a little extra help mastering some of the techniques in this book? QNNtv.com has you covered. In addition to running shows created for traditional television such as *Fons & Porter's Love of Quilting*, *Quilt in a Day with Eleanor Burns*, etc., QNNtv.com produces made-for-QNNtv.com programming such as *Celebrations with Patrick Lose!*, *Quilt Out Loud* with hosts Jodie Davis and Mark Lipinski, and *Quilty with Mary Fons*.

QNNtv.com has a library of over 1,000 quilting videos on-demand, bringing you the most comprehensive quilting library available.

Visit www.shopfonsandporter.com for all your quilting needs.